RV TRAVEL ON A BUDGET: A Mother and Son's Guide to Roadschooling the USA

JUNIPER RIDGE
~ AND ~
ROCKETT RIDGE

CONTENTS

RV TRAVEL ON A BUDGET

ACKNOWLEDGEMENTS

This book would not have been possible without the gentle yet persistent nudging of our good friend, Karin Taylor. She not only provided us with the perfect jumping point for our big adventure, her constant enthusiasm over the years both encourages and sustains our belief in the joys of educational travel. We owe a huge thank you to Kevin Baker for his mechanical genius in keeping our beloved camper van in fine condition. We are deeply indebted to our friend Deb Nam-Krane for her superb writing and editing skills as well as her homeschooling wisdom. We wish to thank Nicki Hagoski-Nye, Adriana Borrero and Nora La Pointe for opening your homes to us for temporary housing when we rolled into town. Rockett has been incredibly fortunate to have the best mentoring in the world from Frank Guidara, Antonio Buehler, Patrick Gunn and Joe Mellen. A special thank you goes to Joanne Rice, Junie Haig, Wynona Ward, Kevin and Kelli O'Donnell, Gary Fletcher and Melissa Moon for sharing the excitement of our adventures. Thank you to Chuck Campbell for putting me on the back of your motorcycle on your way to New Hampshire when I was eleven and introducing me to the joys of the road.

Juniper Ridge

PREFACE

My son, Rockett, and I have been on the road since 2009. Throughout our travels, Rockett has been getting a rich and unique education while I've found satisfying and productive employment. We've both been able to keep in touch with old friends as well as make new ones while we explore the country. Roadschooling continues to be a wonderful adventure for the both of us.

Living on the road isn't for everyone, but if you can make your primary source of income portable, it's a lifestyle within your reach. In the following pages, you will learn our story of how we became a full-time roadschooling family as well as find suggestions for different methods of making a living, homeschooling and modes of travel to meet your family's needs. Some folks hit the road for a short time and others for lengthier periods. Every family has their unique interests, modes of travel and preferences for making the most of life's opportunities. The goal of this book is to help you get started on some learning adventures of your own.

As we meet people throughout our road-schooling journey, we get asked a lot of questions about our lifestyle so we decided to put our experiences together in a book for folks like you who would like to learn more about roadschooling on a budget. Although we have taken several trips outside of the United States, this book will focus on our experiences within the contiguous USA.

Since we are both contributing to this book, we each use a unique font so that you, the reader, can easily recognize whose perspective you are reading. This will be the font when I (mom) speak and Rockett's words will be easily recognized with this font. We both have so much to say about our travels! May you find this book useful for your roadschooling journey, whether it is short or long.

https://juniperandrockettridgeblog.wordpress.com/

Rockett doing his studies

1. WHAT IS ROADSCHOOLING?

*The world is a book and those who do not
travel read only one page. —
Augustine of Hippo*

I magine a child who is permitted to enjoy a field trip every day...what can make for a fuller learning experience than that? Roadschooling is the most natural and exciting way to get a wide-ranging education. When the world is the schoolroom, the opportunity for learning is unlimited. In most school settings, children are expected to learn each subject through a schedule that meets someone else's convenience. There is rarely any allowance to enable a child the freedom to study each subject in the way that catches his or her attention in their unique way. When time constraints are more important than the act of learning, the love and desire to learn are rapidly diminished. Whether you roadschool for ten days, ten months or ten years, doing so will provide a wide range of valuable learning experiences for you and your child/ren that will never be forgotten.

One major advantage of roadschooling is that it increases the odds of fully absorbing a subject into the long-term memory. We all are more likely to retain what we learn when more of our senses are involved in the educational process.[1] For example, whereas most children may learn about the Grand Canyon from a book or video, roadschooling allows the student to learn from personal experience. My son describes when he first discovered the Grand Canyon:

I went to the edge of the cliff and felt the wind rising from the canyon below. And the view from the edge is incredible! In the visitor center, I met people from all over the world around the geography and wildlife displays. In the campground, I smelled the woods surrounding our camper. These are experiences that I will always remember.

There are endless locations across the United States that provide opportunities to meet educational goals. The National Park Service is a fabulous resource for learning about the environment, history and community service. Not only are there 408 recreation areas (currently) to visit, the National Park Service offers a mostly free, educational program that is available in many parks across the country. Rockett is a big fan.

---

[1] http://www.howtolearn.com/2012/12/learning-is-multi-sensory-how-to-engage-all-the-senses-so-children-really-benefit/

Earning a Jr. Ranger badge at a National Park

The Junior Ranger program is an enjoyable learning activity that kids ages five and up can do at participating parks. Each park has a unique booklet that teaches about the animals, plants and the history of the area. Some booklets require the kids to take a tour or attend a lecture where the kids and grownups can learn about paleontology, zoology and even astronomy. Completed booklets are then handed to the ranger and the kids are awarded a badge or patch, and then take a pledge to protect the park. This program is so fun that over 660,000 children participated in it in 2015. Junior Ranger Programs are often available at state parks, too.

The National Park Service logo in stone

Historic sites are just one of the benefits of travel:

For social studies and history, we have visited the homes of famous authors, painters, architects, presidents...the possibilities are endless. When I stand on a bridge and see and smell the water in a moat that surrounds a fort and then explore the fortifications where cannonballs flew, I get the sense that something actually happened there. Need I mention learning about geography? I have spent a lot of time looking at maps, rock formations, mountains, caves and all kinds of waterways. Science is part of everyday experiences when we travel. There is nothing more exciting than seeing wild creatures in their natural habitats, acting as they should. I have seen Florida panthers, wild alligators, friendly manatees and sunbathing crocodiles. North America is full of bears, bobcats, birds and many other species. I especially enjoy seeing animals and reptiles how and where they naturally live.

Wild burros on the side of the road just outside of Las Vegas, Nevada.

I learned to tell time by my mom using the face of a clock to point out sites along the road. "Look...wild burros at 9 o'clock!" I help calculate miles per gallon, time and distance while traveling. We listen to audiobooks and I read books and magazines aloud. Keeping a journal and doing writing projects and workbooks keep me up to date with my learning. One of the things that I think is key for any kind of travel is journaling. Journaling can be done every month, day or week. It's good to write down what happens because you then have it to read back on.

Surf lessons in New Hampshire

Here's the advantage of travel when it comes to getting exercise; you don't have to go to the gym, play soccer or baseball in order to get a workout. You can hike, bike, swim in oceans, rivers and all kinds of places. I have some friends who hiked the Appalachian Trail for a month. Every day they were hiking, swimming, and climbing. I like to play golf and that can be expensive. We decided to volunteer at a state park that had a golf course so I helped clean golf carts and went to play golf at no charge. I like to play a little of each sport.

If your family enjoys team sports, you may want to settle somewhere for the season to participate in a local program. If you are an outdoor person, you will find many places to get a good workout along the way.

The best thing about roadschooling is getting to learn about the things that I am really interested in knowing about. For example, I still like learning about dinosaurs at museums all over, I know how to weave baskets from native grasses, how a lock works, about permaculture gardening, prescribed burns, how to locate an archaeological dig for metal detecting, the reproductive cycle of alligators, finding wild edible plants and how to solder.

Another great learning resource is to look online to check the schedule for children's project workshops that are offered for free at Lowe's and Home Depot stores on weekends. Craft stores also offer all kinds of classes at participating locations such as Michael's and Jo-Ann Fabric and Craft Stores, although some require a fee.

Marine Science Class

If you decide to stay in an area for a few months, your child can join local 4-H clubs, chess clubs, homeschool co-ops, museum classes, volunteer opportunities, music classes or art forums. If you find a comfortable park that you would like to stay in for a few weeks or more, it can be advantageous to get involved with the local community. Whatever the interest, there is usually a cost-effective way to get involved.

2. GOING MOBILE

It is better to travel well than to arrive. –

Buddha

I will never forget the day I first heard about roadschooling. It was the spring of 2009 and I was living in my home in the northwest corner of the United States with my six year-old son, Rockett. I was accustomed to single-parent homeschooling but when I heard the concept of roadschooling from a fellow homeschooler, I got swept away. I spent the next few days seeing images of us exploring the

National Parks, camping by bubbling rivers, driving over mountain ranges and visiting friends across the country. I knew that we had to take this adventure.

At the time I was working part-time as an independent marketing contractor from my home. The work was mobile-friendly: it could be done from anywhere that had a Wi-Fi connection. Sometimes I met with clients in person or kept in touch via email or phone calls. Rockett grew up going almost everywhere I went. After he turned four, I rarely used a sitter. My networking time was spent with individuals, which made it easier to bring him along. Instead of spending money on daycare, I bought several travel-types of toy sets that he was only permitted to play with while he accompanied me to work, so he learned to look forward to my meetings.

Rockett was used to playing quietly while I met with a client at a coffee shop and many of my clients enjoyed meeting him. It was also a great opportunity for him to learn to delay gratification. Once my meeting was over, I would take him someplace fun like a playground to reward him. Overall, he has been a fairly easygoing child who loves to explore new places and has no problem sleeping in different environments. I knew he would adjust easily to life on the road.

Since my son was already homeschooled, I knew I could easily continue with his education. Our homeschooling style leans more toward unschooling in that most of his studies revolve around his interests. In fact, I found that some of the best time to homeschool was in the car; we often sang rhyming math songs and practiced grouping objects while sitting in traffic. The trickier part was figuring out how to downsize from my house to a recreational vehicle (RV) and what it would cost emotionally as well as financially. Could I afford it? Was it safe? Would we get homesick? It would require a big change in lifestyle and an even bigger leap of faith. Over the next few months, I read as much about roadschooling as I could find online before I began my own footwork researching possibilities.

Rockett and I had fun looking at recreational vehicles. He loved climbing up the ladders that led to different types of bunk beds and looking into the little cubby holes for storage that are throughout each vehicle to make the most of every space. Meanwhile, I was evaluating all of the different options. Big fridge or small? Washer/dryer set up? Bath tub? Generator? Slide-outs? I spent several weeks looking at new and used RVs, learning about cleaning the different kinds of holding tanks and exploring financing options.

I was still trying to make up my mind when one day while driving along a back country road I saw a used Ford camper van with a For Sale sign on it. I stopped to take a look and spoke to the owner. The camper was older but very clean and seemed to be just right for us. Rockett fell in love with it immediately. I put a deposit down and had my favorite mechanic look it over. I wound up buying it that week and taking it home.

One benefit of an older vehicle is that the parts tend to be less expensive to replace. This was a huge cost-saver in my case. After having some mechanical improvements done such as replacing brakes, tires, hoses, transmission fluid, etc., we took it for a test trip to the Olympic National Forest to see how everything worked. While camped by a huge lake, we tried everything on it: pulled out the awning over the picnic table at the campsite, figured out the best setting on the fridge, learned how the fresh water storage worked for the sink, spun the front seats around and found hideaways for supplies. We loved it! After that weekend, the ball began to roll full speed.

We couldn't have gone roadschooling without the kindness of our friends. Some helped us move all of our stuff out of the house and into storage. Another let us stay at her home while she was out of the country so we had a cozy place while I waited for the sale of the house and prepared to travel. Yet another friend and her husband said I could store my car at their house. My wonderful friend and mechanic found a used generator for me to buy and he mounted it on the front of the van behind the spare tire. He also installed cat perches up near the ceiling in the van for our kitty. We are incredibly fortunate to have such generous and caring people in our lives!

The biggest challenge at the time was figuring out what to bring that would fit in our camper. I created a system of three categories that Rockett and I sorted everything into: Needs, Wants and Waits. If we had room, the Wants could come along after the Needs had been selected and placed. Once that was accomplished, finding a place for everything to fit into the camper without making it too top heavy determined which Wants would not be left behind. The Waits were put in storage. Rockett was so excited, even sorting our belongings felt like an adventure.

In the evenings, I pored over maps, websites and books to research what places we wanted to explore on our journey. We had no definite travel plan at the time except to take in as many dinosaur exhibits as possible. I figured we would see where that took us and go from there. One family of friends got us started on the right foot; they had learned of a mammoth dig in Washington State and met us there for the first stop on our roadschooling journey. What better way to get started! It was fascinating to see university students working under a paleontologist on a large dig site. When our visit was over, saying goodbye to our friends was particularly difficult. We went down the road to begin our adventure on our own from there.

I have to say that for me, being on the road was a bit scary at first. I used to worry about not having a plan for where I would park each night. It didn't take long, however, before I began to savor not knowing and learned to absorb the joy of living in the moment. I quickly learned to spot safe places to pull into to rest and how to find a safe person to keep an eye on us whenever possible. If there was a spot where other RVs were parked for the night, we would park near each other, like circling the wagons. It felt safe and we would sometimes chat if we ran across each other in the daylight or simply exchange a passing wave to one another while driving away the following morning.

Driving provides time to think. I thought a lot about how humans have been nomads for many thousands of years prior to civilizations being established. Throughout history, nomadic peoples have endured. Although there may be fewer in the world today, there are still many people around the who live on the road while working in carnivals, among fellow gypsies, following herds of animals, and there is a large subculture of people in the United States who move out of their houses and apartments to make their home in an RV. While driving across the states, I would think a lot about the first people who came to North America and what these valleys and landscapes must have been like for them. I felt as though I was sharing some of that experience...except of course, for having to stop for gas every couple of hundred miles.

Before we knew it, days on the road turned into weeks. We fell in love with seeing wonderful sights around the country. The weather itself becomes an integral part of the journey. I remember pointing the sky out to Rockett the first time he saw a rain storm happening in the distance. Rockett was also able to feed his interest in dinosaurs and became quite the dinosaur authority that first year. After several months of being away, we decided not to move back to our home town for a while. I found more marketing work and we continued on our roadschooling journey to visit friends and exciting places.

We stayed connected with our loved ones via

cell phones and email while we traveled. I used to periodically send email updates from the road to everyone. After a while, I started to feel guilty sending what must have seemed like endless vacation news to our friends who were settled in one place most of the time. We still kept in contact but didn't necessarily talk about the adventures. The important part was to maintain the connections. I have to mention that being on the road is certainly not an isolating event. Anytime we want to meet people, we can spend a few nights at a RV park where there is usually an abundance of comrades to visit with and swap travel stories. Most of them are seniors who enjoy spending time with fellow travelers and unless it is a 55+ RV park, kids are often warmly welcomed by the local community. It is not hard to keep a balance of new as well as old friends in our daily lives.

The following year, we flew back to the Northwest and sold most of our belongings. A few kind friends offered to store the boxes of things we could not part with like saddles, favorite books, toys and photos. I got the car out of storage from another friend's home (where would we be without good friends?) and put a roof rack on top of it. We soon hit the road again and spent the next few years traveling off and on: mostly renting space for short periods at campgrounds and RV parks or from friends in between our adventures. In 2014, we decided to roadschool full time, living in our camper van indefinitely without a final destination. In the following pages, you will find reviews of many of the exciting places we have seen. We hope you find them helpful.

3. PLACES TO SEE

THE SOUTHEAST

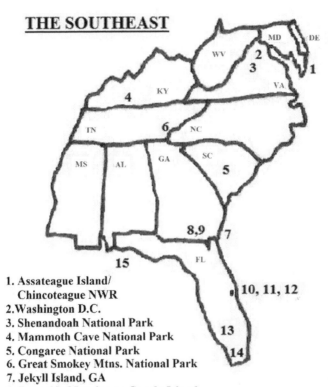

1. Assateague Island/
   Chincoteague NWR
2. Washington D.C.
3. Shenandoah National Park
4. Mammoth Cave National Park
5. Congaree National Park
6. Great Smokey Mtns. National Park
7. Jekyll Island, GA
8. Reynolds Mansion on Sapelo Island
9. Laura S. Walker State Park
10. Okefenokee NWR   13. Skydive Sebastian
11. Florida's Treasure Coast 14. Everglades National Park
12. Kashi Ashram   15. Gulf Islands National Seashore

THE SOUTHEAST

The southeast is full of history, attractive scenery and remarkable people. It has everything from Native American mounds that are thousands of years old to civil rights history museums and lovely beaches. Our first major trip to the southeast was to visit the different kinds of swamps in this part of the country and to hear the mating calls of alligators (see above).

These are some of our favorite places that I think every kid like me would enjoy.

Assateague Island and Chincoteague National Wildlife Refuge

Both of these recreation areas are located right next to each other along the Assateague Island National Seashore. They meet at the border of Virginia and Maryland on the coastal islands. Assateague is in Maryland and Chincoteague is in Virginia.

Wild ponies are on both Chincoteague and Assateague Islands and they are not afraid of anything. These are feral horses that are not owned by anyone. They are protected by the government and they sure know it! They are brown and white and all kinds of colors. A couple of times, the horses came right up to our campsite and they walked to our campfire where we were. Campers are required to stay 100 feet away and we made haste to do so. I was there with some old friends and their mom and we had a great time in the visitor centers, on the beach and in the hole we dug by our campsite. There are many wild birds and bunnies and all kinds of sea creatures in the area. They have a very enjoyable Junior Ranger Program at both visitor centers.

Assateague Island Visitor Center - Maryland District
11800 Marsh View Lane, Berlin, MD 21811
(410)641-1441
http://www.nps.gov/as

Washington D.C.

Yes, you can easily visit our nation's capital with an RV! There are a few parks in the DC area where you can stay for a reasonable price considering that you are near such a big city. We spent a week at Cherry Hill Park Campground and it was super convenient. They not only have all the usual amenities including laundry facilities and a pool, there is a public bus stop in their park that will take you to the subway so you can head into DC. Once there, be prepared to do a lot of walking. We visited many of the Smithsonian Museums (which are free), the Holocaust Museum and several National Monuments. We ducked into the National Archives and looked up some family history, as well. Plan ahead because one week was not enough time to see all there is in DC!

We went to the National Geographic Museum. At the time, there was a Spinosaurus Exhibit that was extremely intriguing. It covered how they found out that Spinosaurus did not walk on two legs like most predators of the dinosaur age, but walked on all fours like an alligator. Its closest relative is the crocodile. They both have a very long, thin snout that is designed to catch fish while swimming. So, this is the only dinosaur that is proven to have spent a majority of its time in the water as opposed to the land and that is one reason why it has a really long tail so it can use it like a crocodile does, to propel itself forward. Spinosaurus is the longest predatory dinosaur of all time!

The National Geographic Museum

https://www.nps.gov/state/dc/index.htm
http://www.cherryhillpark.com/index.cfm

Shenandoah National Park

Located on top of the Blue Ridge Mountain Range is a historic road with spectacular views. There are many places to pull over to see the mountains and the countryside below.

The people who built the road going along the mountain ridge were part of the Civilian Conservation Corps (CCC). They did a lot of useful construction during the depression while FDR was in the White House. We saw two bears along the road while passing through. The only thing that I didn't like about Shenandoah was that if you wanted to camp, you couldn't keep any food, water or Chap Stick in the tent at the campground because of the many black bears in the area! The drive south along the mountain ridges was breathtaking.

Shenandoah National Park
Skyline Dr, Stanley, VA 22851
(540)999-3500
http://www.nps.gov/shen/index.ht

Mammoth Cave National Park

If you like going underground, you will definitely want to visit Mammoth Cave National Park. So far, 400 miles have been found but they are still looking. This is the longest cave system in the world! We signed up for a tour and rode in a bus to the entrance of one cave and went deep down a lot of stairs. Do you see that helmet I'm wearing in the picture? The light really works and that was fun to wear in the dark part of the cave. This was my first time ever seeing stalactites and stalagmites. There were also many different kinds of bugs hanging from the ceilings inside of the caves. There are many more caves to visit here if you have the time. They also have a fun picnic area, streams and trails to explore along with a campground if you want to stay a while.

Mammoth Cave National Park
1 Mammoth Cave Parkway, Mammoth Cave, KY 42259
(270) 758-2180
http://www.nps.gov/maca

Congaree National Park

This was the first stop on our swamp trip. Congaree is located just outside of Columbia, South Carolina (SC). Congaree may look like a swamp but it is a flood plain. The park has a ton of Cypress Trees, the kind that have what are called "knees" sticking up from the ground. Did you know that Spanish Moss is related to pineapples? This spooky-looking stuff that hangs from the trees absorbs food and moisture from the air. We went to Congaree in the spring when it was too cool to see many bugs. We saw turtles, fish, birds and they have a really cool visitor center with a Junior Ranger program. If you plan a trip to get there at the right time of the year, you can see fireflies flash in unison!

Congaree National Park
100 National Park Rd, Hopkins, SC 29061
(803)776-4396
http://www.nps.gov/cong/contacts.htm

Great Smoky Mountains National Park

The most visited National Park in the country; Great Smoky Mountains is unlike any other. The park is known for having more diverse types of animals than are found all over Europe. In fact, while we were there, a gigantic survey was being done to record all the organisms living in the park, from micro-organisms to large plants and animals. The research study is called the All Taxa Biodiversity Inventory (ATBI). It will be interesting to see how many creatures they come up with. Great Smoky Mountains National Park is just stunning and easy to get to from highway 81.

I saw a large, black bear near the road while we drove through the mountains. There were a lot of people at the visitor's center.

Great Smoky Mountains National Park
107 Park Headquarters Rd. Gatlinburg, TN 37738
(865)436-1200
http://www.nps.gov/grsm/contacts.htm

Jekyll Island, Georgia

This island is located along the Golden Isles of the Georgia Coast. It is a great place to explore on your bike. The beach is awesome and the campground is a blast to ride around. They have a sea turtle rescue center with a museum that is worth investigating. There are also many hotels and places to shop and eat. The thing that I did most of time I was there was ride my bike around the campground and I had a good time doing it, too.

(You have to pay a small entrance fee to get on the island.)

http://www.jekyllisland.com/

Reynolds Mansion on Sapelo Island

The mansion was first built in 1810. It was heavily damaged during the civil war but rebuilt in the early 1900s by Howard Coffin, one of the founders of the Hudson Motor Car Company. Then RJ Reynolds of the tobacco family bought it in 1934 and turned it into an entertaining place to live. The basement has a bowling alley and a bar with a pirate theme. On the main level there is a library, a huge dining hall, a front room with paintings of RJ Reynolds and one of Howard Coffin. The top floor has a circus room that you must see. The mansion can be rented for groups of people to stay in its 13 rooms or you can go for lunch and a day tour of Sapelo Island. This is a grand setting for weddings, family reunions or hide and go seek. You have to make reservations and take a nice ferry ride out to the island. Reynolds Mansion is an enchanting place to visit.

R.J. Reynolds Mansion on Sapelo Island
Sapelo Island, GA
(912)485-2299
http://gastateparks.org/lodges/reynolds/about/

Laura S. Walker State Park

Located right at the tip of the Okefenokee Swamp in southeast Georgia, this attractive park offers a golf course, boating, camping, animal hikes on Saturday afternoons and an interpretive center with two baby alligators. It has two playgrounds: one near the water and the other in the campground. I like the one near the water best because it has more things to do. They have super knowledgeable rangers running the park. There are cabins for rent that you can stay in and they are really cool. They also have a bridge that goes across the lake where you can walk. If you shine a light in the lake at night, you can sometimes see alligator eyes reflecting back at you from the water. If you decide to go for a walk along one of the trails, you might run across a gopher tortoise - the Georgia State reptile – they are brown and dig holes really fast.

This is a great place to camp, especially if you plan on visiting different sides of the Okefenokee Swamp.

Laura S. Walker State Park
5653 Laura Walker Rd., Waycross, GA 31503
(912)287-4900
http://gastateparks.org/LauraSWalker

Canoeing in the Okefenokee Swamp on our quest to hear the mating calls of alligators.

Okefenokee National Wildlife Refuge
The Okefenokee National Wildlife Refuge is located in the southeast part of Georgia near the border of Florida. It is so big that it has three different entrances.

While we were in the Okefenokee Swamp, we saw so many gators that it got to where my mom would say "alligator!" and I wouldn't even bother to look up from whatever I was doing. Did you know that alligators can stay underwater for up to 30 minutes? The swamp water there looks black and really murky due to the tannins from plants in the water.

There are three different entrances to Okefenokee: one is the National Wildlife Refuge (NWR) at the East entrance in Folkston, Stephen C. Foster State Park is on the west side and the third is Okefenokee Swamp Park, a commercially run enterprise at the northern tip of the swamp. The NWR has the best visitor center and they offer a high-quality junior ranger program. Growing in the swamp is a plant material that looks like land but actually covers the water surface and in some places, it is able to hold a human's weight. Okefenokee is the Indian term for trembling earth. The plant layer above the water periodically moves as a result of decaying matter. They have a replica of it in the visitor center and it really does tremble!

Since we were there as part of our swamp trip, we got up early one morning to rent a canoe then headed out into the swamp where we heard alligator mating calls. The sounds make you imagine that the water is erupting and what you might think that the call of a T-rex would sound like. It's very prehistoric sounding!

The Stephen C. Foster State Park entrance offers a fabulous swamp boat tour experience that explains a lot. Camping is available near the entrance, as are platforms deep in the swamp where you can paddle a canoe out to camp overnight. You will see a wealth of creatures in the wild just wandering around the boat dock there. We saw huge turtles, lizards, birds, fish and of course a bunch of alligators lounging in the sun.

The north entrance is privately owned, very commercial and only for day use. I recommend skipping that entrance but definitely visiting the other two as they offer different views of the swamp and both are well worth it! You also get to see a lot of the area when you drive from one side to the other. You will never forget Okefenokee Swamp!

Okefenokee National Wildlife Refuge
2700 Suwannee Canal Road, Folkston, GA 31537.
(912)496-7836
http://www.fws.gov/refuge/okefenokee/

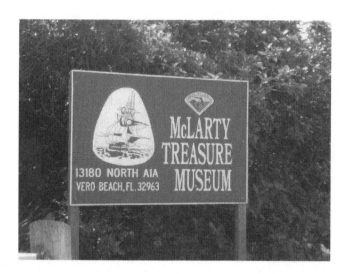

The Treasure Coast of Florida

They weren't kidding when they named this part of Florida "The Treasure Coast." In centuries past, Spanish ships carrying jewels and riches that were headed for Europe continually sunk along that coast due to hurricanes and the treacherous coastline. Since then, people still find treasure after a storm. But the area is a treasure for another reason; there is all this wildlife in the area. There are many campgrounds and public beaches where you can park and enjoy watching dolphins, pelicans, sea snails, sea turtles and the many birds who come to feast! On the other side of the bridge there is another campground and it has these little sites near the water where you can camp, boat, swim, fish and any other thing you want to do. There is a state beach nearby that has almost no people there most of the time and you can swim with manatees. When me and my mom were in a spot that was up to my chest all these fish jumped out of the water to get away from something and one hit me square in the chest! The McLarty Treasure Museum has displays about the people that made the discovery of some of the Spanish ships that sunk right there. One of the treasure hunters is shown in a video telling the story of how his wife hated him treasure hunting all of the time on the beach until one day, he brought an emerald ring about the size of a quarter home to her and she didn't complain ever again. It also tells how the ships got to where they are now and catches you up on the continued search for lost treasure.

Kashi Ashram in Florida

If you happen to be near Sebastian, Florida and are in the mood for spiritual worship, this is the perfect place for the traveler of any faith to stop. Kashi is a multi-religion spiritual community with beautiful grounds that have statues and many sacred spaces for practically every faith! It is open to the public and offers free tours.

Not only did I have an enjoyable time walking their intricate labyrinth, I met their Swami (the manager of the Ashram), a really kind guy who told me about growing up at Kashi when he spent his nights in a tree house with air conditioning. There are lovely gardens everywhere around the Ashram. On the weekends, they sell fresh, organic vegetables and they offer Saturday lunches that are very tasty. I still think that the ginger salad dressing they have is the best ever!

Kashi Ashram
11155 Roseland Rd., Sebastian, FL 32958
(772)589-1403
http://www.kashi.org

Skydive Sebastian
If you like seeing people falling in the air, you will want to stop by here for some exciting skydiving action. There is an outdoor café where you can sit, have lunch and watch skydivers from all over the world float down from the sky above you to land on the runway by the cafe.

Sometimes you'll look up and what look like tiny balloons way up high in the sky, turn out to be a group of people falling together. I actually had an interview with one of the pilots who I learned a lot from and he had some really funny stories to tell. The age limit for skydiving is 18 and you have to be an experienced diver in order to jump out of a plane. If you happen to be in the area, it is a really exciting thing to do to watch people fall from the sky.

Skydive Sebastian
400 Airport Dr W., Sebastian, FL 32958
(772)388-5672
http://www.skydiveseb.com

W.P. Franklin Lock and Dam
Situated along the Okeechobee Waterway, W.P. Franklin Lock has many fun activities to enjoy.

If you have a boat, you can go through the lock. If you don't, you can go up onto the walkway by the lock to watch how it operates. If you're lucky, you might see some manatees or an alligator going through! There is also a beach on one side where you can safely swim with the alligators. There are so many gorgeous and exotic birds and fish along the Okeechobee, it's really fun to just sit in the water and see who comes by. There is a large playground with many picnic areas and a campground across the water. They have a visitor center that shows a film about the area and has interactive exhibits that teach about the environment and the waterway. I would definitely recommend stopping in for the day or camping here.

W.P. Franklin Lock and Dam
17850 N Franklin Lock Rd., Alva, FL 33920
(239)694-8770
http://www.recreation.gov/camping/wp-franklin

Everglades National Park
This park is the largest protected wilderness region on the east side of the Mississippi River. It is known for a

great spot to see striking birds such as Roseate Spoonbills. They are a bright pink color. I saw about 100 of them in a tree in Southern Florida. At one point, they were almost hunted to extinction because their beautiful feathers were used to make women's hats. In the water, you will find Gars; a type of fish with a really long snout. Some are black, green or brown. This is also the only place in the world where you can see alligators and crocodiles in the same habitat. There are large manatees hanging around the dock at the south end, which are over 12 feet long! Before you go, do not enter the Everglades without some powerful bug repellent and soother. The no-see-ems are ferocious and can come in through a screen window! This is one park that cannot be missed.

Everglades National Park
40001 State Rd. 9336, Homestead, FL 33034-6733
(305)242-7700
http://www.nps.gov/ever/contacts.htm

A visit from some manatees at Everglades National Park

Gulf Islands National Seashore

The panhandle of Florida provides a unique experience not found in the rest of the state. Not surprisingly, a different ocean makes for an exceptional coastal experience. The long, white beaches of the Gulf Coast are lovely. We stopped to pitch a tent at this pretty campground near the beach. It offers many trails, pretty beaches and has a spectacular fort along with a visitor center.

Fort Pickens was really fun to explore. It had endless rooms to stroll through and a gigantic platform where an old cannon could rotate. We walked along a trail here and that's when I first learned about Ospreys. They are intelligent raptors who build their nests at the top of dead trees. You can easily see them since there are no leaves to block the view of their nests.

Gulf Islands National Seashore
1801 Gulf Breeze Pkwy, Gulf Breeze, FL 32563
(850)934.2600
https://www.nps.gov/guis/index.htm

THE NORTHEAST

2, 3 -Boston/Cambridge

6, 7, 8 -New York City

1. The Derby Line Library
2. Tea Party Museum
3. Harvard Museum of Natural History
4. Sturbridge Village
5. Farm Sanctuary in New York State
6. The Statue of Liberty
7. Ellis Island Immigration Museum
8. New York City

THE NORTHEAST

T he Northeast portion of the United States has loads of history, colorful autumn scenery, billowy snow to ski in and plenty of culture to be explored. Whether you take pleasure in the city life of New York or enjoy strolling the coastal beaches of Maine, you will find no end of exciting places to visit and delightful accents to intrigue a young listener's ears.

Standing on the border of Canada and the USA

The Derby Line Library

If you find yourself near the top of Vermont by the Canadian border, this charming and unique library has the distinction of being located in two different countries. It even has a line on the floor designating the exact border.

Yes, you can actually stand in two nations at once! The

library has books in both English and French and the people who work there are bilingual as well. This is one way to cross the border without a passport.

Be sure to check the hours before you go.

The Derby Line Library
93 Caswell Ave, Derby Line, VT 05830
(802) 873-3022

Tea Party Museum

Boston is known for its many historic sites. If you haven't time to see them all, be sure to visit the Tea Party Museum on Boston's waterfront. Here is your opportunity to dump tea in the Boston Harbor just like the Sons of Liberty did in 1773...really. They put on a lively reproduction of the Tea Party Revolt that is super fun. People in period costumes tell you about what was going on at the time in Boston and let you become an actor in their troupe so you get a feather to put in your hair   or   hat.

They like you to play a role that includes being able to go outside, yell and throw "tea crates" overboard into the harbor. (They are actually foam blocks that have string tied through them so they can pull them back up afterward.). I really had a good time at this event. And the cool thing is that a lot of the activity takes place on an actual boat!

Tea Party Museum Boston, MA
306 Congress St, Boston, MA 02210
(617) 338-1773
http://www.bostonteapartyship.com

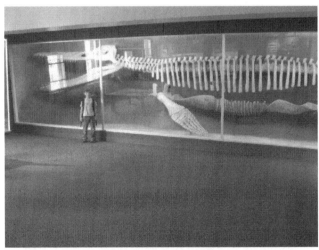

A Kronosaurus skeleton at the Harvard Museum of Natural History

Harvard Museum of Natural History

Located at the famous University, here is where you can find practically a little bit of everything under the sun, including deer with tusks.

This museum has three parts to it: the mineralogical and geological section, the botanical museum and the zoological building. You will find loads of preserved animal and plant species, as well as a large cultural section. I was impressed when I walked into a room to find a skeleton of a Kronosaurus along an entire wall! They also have a rare preserved body of a coelacanth. They have a gigantic room full of insects, another full of sea creatures and another still with African animals. They even have skeletons of whales hanging from the ceiling! The whole place is just really cool.

Harvard Museum of Natural History
26 Oxford St, Cambridge, MA 02138
(617)495-3045
http://hmnh.harvard.edu

Sturbridge Village

About two hours west of Boston is Sturbridge, Massachusetts, where you will find a village that is a living replica of life in the eighteenth and nineteenth centuries. Every person who works there dresses and plays the part of residents who lived there at the time. There are shops with workers who demonstrate their craft, homes with residents who show you how they prepare food, there are domestic animals that are being tended to and special workshops open to the public to learn handy things such as candle making.

When I was in the tinsmith's shop, a visiting school child threw a stone through the window and broke the glass. I learned that children back then would probably be running the farm, not breaking windows. This is definitely a lively and hands on place to visit if you're traveling in Western Massachusetts. Watch the windows if you go.

Sturbridge Village
1 Old Sturbridge Village Rd, Sturbridge, MA 01566
(508)347-3362
https://www.osv.org/content/directions

Farm Sanctuary in New York State

One of the most valuable aspects of travel is being able to see the economic means of the country. Not only have we stopped to look at different fields of crops growing such as corn, soy and cotton, we have learned about factory farming. Farm Sanctuary is a non-profit animal rescue shelter dedicated to ending the cruelty of factory farming. They have been going strong since 1986 to protect farm animals. This is the first farm animal shelter established in the United States.

They have over 500 rescued animals there including factory farmed pigs, sheep, chickens, goats and cattle (among other animals that are raised for profit) plus they provide good homes for them and find adoptive parents. They are open to the public and have displays for educating people about what is involved with factory farming. We went to one of their Hoe Downs one year and listened to many people talk about the impact of diet upon animal welfare, human health and the environment. Although they have three locations, one in New York and two in California, the one in NY is where we went. It is a beautiful farm where the animals all seemed very healthy, happy and well cared for.

Farm Sanctuary National Headquarters
3100 Aikens Road, Watkins Glen, NY 14891
(607)583-2225
http://www.farmsanctuary.org/the-sanctuaries/watkins-glen-ny/

The Statue of Liberty
There are few statues in the United States that you can climb up into and see a view of the greatest city on Earth. Although it is fairly easy to get to the island and up to the pedestal, getting to the crown can be tricky. I was able to go to the pedestal where they give you electronic handsets that you can listen to while touring the museum to learn about the statue. The

museum below the statue has a very informational display on her history. France gave this copper statue to the United States as a gift of friendship. It represents democracy and freedom. In 1924, it was made a National Monument. There are some displays that are really funny. If you want to go up into the crown, you may want to make reservations ahead of time, possibly months before you go.

The Statue of Liberty
(212) 363-3200
http://www.nps.gov/stli

Ellis Island Immigration Museum
An easy hop from the Statue of Liberty is Ellis Island. Twelve million immigrants came through here when they first arrived in the United States between 1892 and 1924. It would take anywhere from 3 to 7 hours for each person to get processed.

The building is set up well for showing what it was like

to come to this country. They show how the quick physical exams were done and how people decided where to settle. The museum has a lot of photo displays to wander through. Heads up: if you are looking for information on a relative, they do not keep records here. (My grandmother came through Ellis Island but we could not find out anything there. We later did in Washington DC.)

Ellis Island Visitor Center
(212)363-3200
http://www.nps.gov/elis/index.htm

New York City
New York City is definitely a must-see but not particularly RV-friendly. When we visit the area, we either stay with friends or park our camper and grab a room across the water in nearby Newark, New Jersey.

Staying in Newark is MUCH less expensive than New York and is a short train ride away. It's interesting to experience the commuter railway with so many people who do it every day. The subway system in town is also convenient as it makes it easy to get around Manhattan, where we spent most of our time. We visited museums, Times Square, Wall Street, Central Park, Greenwich Village, the Empire State Building and some great restaurants.

New York City is a hopping place. I had a great time seeing Rockefeller Center and just walking around this great city. I walked with my Mom to the Lego Store in Rockefeller Center and it was amazing in there! They had Lego dragons on the ceiling and a gigantic Lego display in the store window. I also liked the Museum of Natural History, especially their prehistoric displays. One of the most fun things we did was to walk the Highline. It's an old raised train track that was made into a beautiful walkway that is above the streets and filled with gardens and plants and cool benches to sit on. I liked looking down at all the buildings and streets from above without having to worry about traffic. At one end, you can stop and have a snack at an outside restaurant.

http://www.nycgo.com/

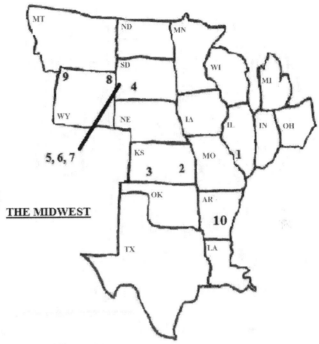

THE MIDWEST

1. Cahokia Mounds
2. Tall Grass Prairie National Park
3. Fort Larned National Historic Site
4. Badlands National Park
5. Crazy HOrse Memorial
6. Mt. Rushmore National Memorial
7. Black Hills Institute of Geological Research
8. Devils Tower National Monument
9. Yellowstone National Park
10. Hot Springs, AR

A Madonna of the Trail Statue honors mothers that cared for children along the Wagon Trail

THE MIDWEST

W hether you track the Wagon Trail that that tens of thousands of people followed on the move west during the nineteenth century or you meander across the Mississippi River or ancient Indian Mounds and cities, there are many exceptional places to visit throughout the central states. If you enjoy seeing open prairies, marvelous mountain sculptures or hidden caves, there are many outlets to enjoy both natural and man-made spectacles. Don't forget to take pictures.

Cahokia Mounds

Easily accessed from Interstate 70 on the East side of St. Louis, there is a fabulous Native American Museum that is one of our favorite places in this country. Cahokia Mounds at one time supported close to 20,000 people. It was a bigger city than London in 1250 CE. Although many of the mounds have been leveled, there are still many left with some large ones to wander amongst plus a wooden version of Stonehenge that the people at the visitor center call "Woodhenge." Inside their museum, you will find life-size dioramas, interactive displays and a movie that I will never forget. Outside, you are able to go on the mounds, many of which haven't been excavated. Cahokia is a UNESCO (United Nations Environment Science and Cultural Organization) World Heritage Site; it is a memorable and important historical place to visit.

Cahokia Mounds
Collinsville, IL
(618)346-5160
http://www.cahokiamounds.org/

Photo courtesy of National Park Service

Tall Grass Prairie National Park

The Tall Grass Prairie National Park is a very special site in the Flint Hills of Kansas. It is one of the few places left in the country where the land is exactly as it looked when the wagon trains went through before the country was cleared and re-settled by New Americans (mostly of European descent.) There were once 170 million acres of open plains but less than 4% of that land is left today, mostly here in this park. The visitor center is particularly interesting as the building is very old.

Once inside, they show a film all about the area. There are several restored buildings that you can explore and see what life used to be like on the open prairie with fine detail. When we were there, it was hot out so we brought our cat inside with us in a cloth cat carrier. Nobody noticed that it wasn't a purse my mom was carrying. Our kitty did not make a peep and she sat quietly with us while we watched the video and then walked around the buildings. This fascinating park provides trails to be hiked and great views to be seen.

This is the perfect place for learning about how the plains used to be, especially for young pioneers.

Tall Grass Prairie National Preserve Visitor Center
2480B KS Hwy 177, Strong City, KS 66869
(620)273-8494
http://www.nps.gov/tapr/planyourvisit/index.htm

Fort Larned National Historic Site
The troops stationed at Fort Larned were called "The Guardians of the Santa Fe Trail." This fort was very important from the 1860's to the 1870's as that was during the height of the Indian Wars. It later was used as a trading post where both Indians and settlers sold and/or traded much of their wares. A visit here will allow you to go through the original fort that is very well-preserved.

I had a fun time exploring Fort Larned. The downstairs has all these rooms you can go through. There are raised walkways up above that run along the walls and I could look out over the prairie. There is also a tepee and cannon. We got there late one night and parked outside the entrance. While we had breakfast, the park opened and it made for a fun way to start the day. This is definitely a great place to visit.

Fort Larned National Historic Site
1767 Kansas Hwy 156, Larned, KS 67550-9321
(620)285-6911
http://www.nps.gov/fols/contacts.htm

Badlands National Park
The French weren't kidding when they named this area the "Bad Lands to Cross." The area draws visitors from all over the world thanks to the rugged landscape. Badlands National Park is 244,000 acres of protected land made up of prairie and mountainous terrain. There are many piles of sediment sticking up out of the ground and there are many gorges as well as valleys. If you drive through the park you can stop for

scenic views to admire the eye-catching sites and look for pinnacles, bison and prairie dogs. Because of such diversity in the landscape it makes for a great place to look for prehistoric mammal fossils such as the saber-toothed cat.

Badlands National Park
25216 Ben Reifel Road, Interior, SD 57750
(605) 433-5361
http://www.nps.gov/badl/contacts.htm

Crazy Horse Memorial
The largest sculpture in the world is being built in honor of Sioux Leader Crazy Horse. Not long after Mt. Rushmore was completed, Oglala Lakota Chief Henry Standing Bear met with the sculptor of Mt. Rushmore, Korczak Ziolkowski, to ask him to help with a mountain-sized memorial to honor all North American Indians. This gigantic sculpture of Crazy Horse riding a horse was started in 1947 and is still being worked on today.

I am glad to see such a historical sculpture in the works. I wish they could hurry it up so we could see the part with the horse!

Crazy Horse Memorial
12151 Avenue of the Chiefs, Crazy Horse, SD 57730
https://crazyhorsememorial.org

Mt. Rushmore National Memorial

Talk about a lot of work! I could not imagine carving faces on cliffs for a living. Did you know that it took 400 workers 14 years to complete this sculpture? They finished in 1941. It's fascinating to walk around and see them from below. These 4 presidents look very real up on the cliffs. Three million visitors stop by here every year.

Mount Rushmore National Memorial
13000 Hwy 244 Bldg 31 Ste 1, Keystone, SD 57751
(605) 574-2523

http://www.nps.gov/moru/index.htm

Black Hills Institute of Geological Research

The Black Hills Institute is a particularly interesting facility as they provide many museums and collectors with paleontological excavations, cast replicas and professionally prepared fossils. The building itself is located in town, so if you have a larger vehicle, you may need to find back street parking.

I love this museum. It has the best display of dinosaur fossils I have ever seen. When I was there, they had a complete skeleton of a Tyrannosaurus Rex (as you can see in the picture) and a skeleton of a dunkleosteus (prehistoric fish) as well as many other skeletons. They had a hands-on display with a few hammers and chisels where the kids could work at excavating some fossils from cement. It was really fun.

Black Hills Institute of Geological Research, Inc.
117 Main St, Hill City, SD 57745
(605) 574-3919
http://www.bhigr.com

Devils Tower National Monument
Dedicated the first National Monument ever in 1906, Devils Tower is one of nature's most astonishing geologic formations. Although it may look man made, it actually is the result of a fountain of lava that came out of the ground 60 million years ago. Over 850 feet tall, it has long been a sacred site for the Lakota and other local tribes. The tower has unique cracks in the hundreds that attract rock climbers from all over.

There is a trail that you can take to walk all around Devils Tower. I could hardly stop looking up! There were tons of people coming in buses to see it as well. We stopped at the picnic tables to have lunch. As we left, we saw lots of prairie dogs along the side of the road. We stopped to watch them play among their holes for a while. It was a great day.

Devils Tower National Monument
P.O. Box 10, Devils Tower, WY 82714-0010
(307)467-5283
http://www.nps.gov/deto/contacts.htm

Bison grazing in the distance at Yellowstone

Yellowstone National Park

Did you know that Yellowstone was designated the first National Park in the United States? In fact, back in the 1800s (when this happened), nobody would come see it because the settlers were afraid of the nine Native

American tribes living in the area. To alleviate the anxiety, the park development folks started a rumor saying that it was safe to visit because the Native Americans were afraid of the geysers (and apparently, the newcomers bought this ridiculous story). Anyway, there is good reason why Yellowstone was the first National Park; it has so much rare beauty that is hard to find elsewhere!

You will see many geysers that shoot hot water over 90 feet into the air at regular intervals. There are loads of animals that you see along the roads including bears, bison and elk. Yellowstone is the size of Rhode Island and is located in two different states: Montana and Wyoming. I just love those geysers. We stopped at the side of the road at one point and sat by a tiny water hole that had steaming water in it.

There are huge waterfalls and open meadows with trees that seem to go on forever. There are cabins that can be rented but you will want to plan ahead if you wish to go during the busy season.

Yellowstone National Park
PO Box 168, Yellowstone National Park, WY 82190
(307)344-7381
http://www.nps.gov/yell

Hot Springs, Arkansas

Underground water provides a unique history for this fancy little town. Before Europeans settled here, the Indians used the springs for rituals. Later, the French used the water for healing and the practice continues to this day. We walked downtown along Bath House Row where you can find structures that are over 100 years old and still open for bathing. Unfortunately, they did not permit minors to use them while we were there, so we didn't get a chance to dip into a true, hot springs bath. We did however, enjoy visiting the city and checked out a public fountain or two. There is also Hot Springs National Park to explore.

http://www.hotsprings.org/

THE SOUTHWEST

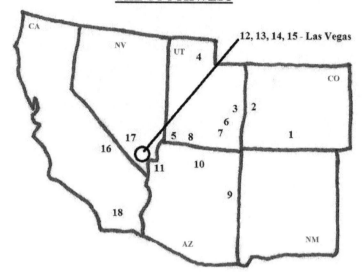

1. Great Sand Dunes National Park
2. Museum of Western Colorado
3. Sego Canyon Petroglyphs
4. Odgen's Eccles Dinosaur Park
5. Zion National Park
6. Arches National Park
7. Canyonlands National Park
8. Best Friends Animal Sanctuary
9. Petrified Forest National Park

10. Grand Canyon
11. Lake Mead National Recreation Area
12. Las Vegas Natural History Museum
13. Springs Preserve
14. Aliante Nature Discovery Park
15. Red Rock Canyon
16. Death Valley National Park
17. Devils Hole National Wildlife Refuge
18. Joshua Tree National Park

THE SOUTHWEST

I f you love extremes, this is the part of the country for you. You can explore cool, tall mountains and hot, low deserts. In the winter, you find desert cactus wildflowers blooming among cacti of all shapes and sizes. In the mountains there are spectacular trails and views of lovely colors across the horizon. And so many canyons to be explored! It is surprising how an area can be so hot during the day then cold at night. And that dry land can have flash floods come suddenly crashing through the desert. Some of our favorite spots are in the National Parks of the great southwest.

Great Sand Dunes National Park in Southern Colorado

Located in the southeast part of Colorado, this National Park provides an unforgettable experience. Here are the tallest sand dunes in the country...and it's nowhere near an ocean!

Great Sand Dunes National Park has dunes over 750 feet tall. When you're there, you feel like you're in the middle of the Sahara Desert. Except for the forest at the base of the mountains where you can camp, it seems like there is no end to the mounds of sand all around you. You might wonder how all that sand gets piled up in the middle of the country, in Colorado of all places! It is so cool...there is even a river running around some of the sand dunes where you can swim. We haven't met a lot of people that have been here. I think all kids should come here.

Great Sand Dunes National Park
11500 Highway 150, Mosca, CO 81146-9798

(719)378-6399
http://www.nps.gov/grsa/contacts.htm

The Museum of Western Colorado: Dinosaur Journey

I loved this museum! It is really exciting, thanks to the robotic dinosaurs. The robots are so lifelike! I remember walking around the exhibits and seeing one Allosaurus eating meat. Then we came around a corner and we saw a Dilophosaurus that spits water at you when you walk by! (The real Dilophosaurus didn't really spit water or venom but ever since the movie Jurassic Park came out, people think it did. Also, it is smaller in the movies than it actually was, closer to 20 feet tall, not three feet.) They also had a film you could watch about dinosaurs and a large exhibit that shows how fossils are preserved.

This museum is well worth the visit if you are traveling through western Colorado, especially if you have a dinosaur fanatic in your midst.

The Museum of Western Colorado: Dinosaur Journey
550 Jurassic Court, Fruita, CO 81521.
(970) 858-7282
http://www.museumofwesternco.com

Sego Canyon Petroglyphs

This just goes to show how many petroglyphs there are around the United States. We found this unlikely site right off the highway 70 in Sego Canyon, Utah, which is about 50 miles west of the Colorado-Utah state line. It is so easy to hop off of the highway to go a few miles north and find yourself in a canyon that has ancient, lifelike paintings on the rock walls. At Sego Canyon you will view artwork of three distinct cultures from different time periods. The detail on the petroglyphs is fascinating. It is a very special place to stop if you enjoy Native American art and history.

Ogden's George S. Eccles Dinosaur Park
If you have a dinosaur enthusiast in your family, this is a must-see. Not only is there a museum with life-sized dinosaur exhibits inside, there is a huge park outdoors with many gigantic prehistoric dinosaurs that seem very realistic out in nature. You will walk among those that appear to be in battle as well as dinosaurs enjoying the water. There is also a playground and a great gift shop with dinosaur films playing. This park is so cool!

Ogden's George S. Eccles Dinosaur Park
1544 East Park Boulevard, Ogden, UT 84401
(801) 393-DINO
http://www.dinosaurpark.org

Zion National Park

People have lived in Zion for over 6,000 years. Open year round, Zion is hot and crowded in the summer so you will likely leave your car in the parking lot then ride the courtesy bus into the park. If you go in the winter, you can drive your vehicle through on your own and it is just as beautiful, especially seeing the red rock covered with clean snow. You can also hike along the valley and follow a stream into a canyon.

There are pools along the stream and it is a very peaceful place to visit. When you drive through the park and up the side of one cliff, it is such a steep drop off that it seems like you are going to fall off the edge. Then when you get to the top you go into a tunnel with open views and you can see the valley below from there. I will never forget that tunnel. They also have a really good Jr. Ranger program at Zion.

Zion National Park

Springdale, UT 84767
(435)772-3256
http://www.nps.gov/zion/index.htm

Arches National Park
This is a great location for taking photos of bright red rock formations. Here you will find more than 2,000 arches formed by natural erosion. We walked a trail and saw some really big boulders balanced on top of smaller rock pedestals. They look like they will roll right off at any moment. I first started participating in the Junior Ranger Program when I was at Arches and I learned a ton!

Arches National Park
PO Box 907, Moab, UT 84532-907
(435) 719-2299
http://www.nps.gov/arch/index.htm

Canyonlands National Park

Not far from Arches National Park is Canyonlands. With its many trails to explore and unforgettable canyons to view, Canyonlands will enchant you. One trail takes you over rocks that you scale by going up a ladder and there are several locations where people lived beneath overhanging ledges in years past. Were they looking for gold? Hiding from the authorities? It is definitely Old West stuff. We drove through a large part of the area and spent the night near the southern portion of the park. The quiet beauty of Canyonlands is magnificent.

I will always remember walking a trail and coming upon "Newspaper Rock," which has loads of petroglyphs and ancient markings! They also have a fun Jr. Ranger Program there.

Perusing Newspaper Rock at Canyonlands National Park

Canyonlands National Park
2282 SW Resource Blvd. Moab, UT 84532
(435) 719-2313
http://www.nps.gov/cany/index.htm

Best Friends Animal Sanctuary in Southern Utah

Do you remember the news about when NFL quarterback player, Michael Vick was caught using his dogs to make money on dogfights? This is where those dogs went for recovery. Best Friends Animal Sanctuary is by far the most beautiful animal shelter we have ever seen. Not only is it on a huge piece of lovely property, they offer opportunities to come visit, volunteer, tour and even spend the night with animals who need adopting. Here you can adopt pigs, cats, dogs, horses and other types of animals. Housing is available to rent so that you can "live" with your potential new companion before taking her/him home. They also welcome volunteers to come work with the animals. All of the potential adoptees look like they are well taken care of as they live in buildings that are specially set up for their particular species.

We volunteered to work with the cats and they looked really happy climbing around on the cat trees in the buildings.

The horses had plenty of room to enjoy their surroundings and when we stopped by at Dogtown, the canines were obviously well taken care of; it was very touching. The property is in a breathtakingly stunning part of southern Utah. Best Friends offers a super tour of all of their buildings. You can enjoy a delicious lunch there by a spectacular view. It is definitely worth going out of your way to see a shelter so obviously designed with love for animals. You may want to arrange a tour in advance.

Best Friends Animal Sanctuary
5001 Angel Canyon Road Kanab, Utah 84741-
435-644-2001
http://www.bestfriends.org

Photo courtesy of National Park Service

Petrified Forest National Park
If you enjoy looking at geological wonders, this is the place for you.

There are lots of pieces of petrified wood to walk amongst. I figure that they must have come from very large trees by the size of these spectacular rocks.

What is surprising about this park is that even though there are lots of specimens to see, the place is in a part of Arizona that is far from any forest. The Painted Desert has many colors to see. When you get to the visitor center you will find that they have an excellent map of the area on a table that has the mountains and all geographical details on it. The park is also great for people who like looking at replicas of prehistoric creatures. When we were there, the Jr. Ranger Program offered a really cool badge and patch to choose from.

Petrified Forest National Park
1 Park Road, Petrified Forest, AZ 86028
(928)524-6228
http://www.nps.gov/pefo/contacts.html

The Grand Canyon in Arizona

If you are traveling through Arizona at all, it is definitely worth the time to go a little out of your way to visit the Grand Canyon. You will never forget the breathtaking views. From the edge of the canyon you can see the different layers of sediments that show the history of past environments.

Over 5 million visitors a year come to see the Grand Canyon. Some folks sign up for a week long boat trip along the Colorado River that you look down upon from the edge. It looks really tiny from so high up! It's mind boggling to think that the Colorado River and rainwater carved out these gigantic caverns in the earth. The canyon is 277 miles long and at one place it is 18 miles wide! They have a really great Junior Ranger Program there. One ranger gave a presentation on animal scat and put one in his mouth! He later said it wasn't real, only made of rubber. Yuck. We camped there one Fourth of July and didn't hear any fireworks, only owls.

Grand Canyon National Park
Grand Canyon, AZ 86023
(928)638-7888
http://www.nps.gov/grca/index.ht

Lake Mead National Recreation Area

I will never forget going to Lake Mead in Arizona. Once there, it's really surprising to see such a large body of water way out in the desert. (If you go to nearby Hoover Dam, you will understand how the lake got there.) The hills surrounding the lake are a wonder to look at. I learned a lot about how much of Lake Mead goes to supplying Las Vegas with water and how that is a big concern for the future. A surprising thing is that I would never expect that to find seagulls by the lake since it is freshwater and quite a ways from the Pacific Ocean, but amazingly there are! I earned a Jr. Ranger badge at the visitor center. I will never forget how the ranger put some goat horns on my head.

Lake Mead National Recreation Area
Temple Bar Marina, AZ 86443
(702) 293-8990
www.nps.gov/lake/planyourvisit/directions.htm

Las Vegas, Nevada

When I first went to Las Vegas and thought of what the strip would look like, I imagined a strip of pink and green light stretching down a highway through the city. I was very much surprised when there was no pink and green strip, but instead, I saw that all the hotels and casinos had giant fountains, statues and huge structures with lights. I found a lot more to see here.

Las Vegas Natural History Museum

Las Vegas has much more to offer besides gambling. It has a spectacular imitation of the King Tut collection that used to be in one of the casinos. The museum was very grateful to be able to display it. It was so well done, I never would have guessed it wasn't real!

They also have some rooms with animal exhibits with marvelous dioramas of the African animals like the lions and such. They are well known for their dinosaur section and do a good job explaining different types of dinosaur periods. I had seen so many dinosaur museums by the time we got there that I had become a snob about dinosaur exhibits. Looking back, this museum isn't bad. I suggest that you go there before doing the Dinosaur Diamond if you have that planned. (The Dinosaur Diamond is a section of the United States where many dinosaur bones have been discovered.)

Las Vegas Natural History Museum
900 Las Vegas Blvd N, Las Vegas, NV 89101
(702)384-346
http://www.lvnhm.org/

Springs Preserve
Conveniently located in Las Vegas, this combination park and museum has something for everyone. One can spend days looking at all the fascinating things to see.

The really interesting thing about Springs Preserve is that it has the first water source that was used when Las Vegas was first established. One room has a glass floor where you can see flashing, multicolored lights under the water highlighting the actual spring. In the gift shop, there is a glass floor and under it there is a Gila monster and a diamond back rattle snake in a tunnel together. They look like they are about to fight! There are museums with changing exhibits, with live animals and a building with local Las Vegas history.

There is another building that has information about conserving energy, recycling and lots to learn about environmental concerns. There are loads of games and learning tools for children of all ages. One thing about it is that when you start to enter they have these little rivers that you are able to play in and watch the dragonflies. In one museum, they have a lively flash flood exhibit in a small room with a platform above a stream that you will never forget! There are lovely gardens to explore and you can rent bikes there as well. They even have a small library there. There is a great restaurant at the top of one building where you can sit outside on the deck and look over the top of Las Vegas. I just love Springs Preserve!

Springs Preserve
333 S Valley View Blvd, Las Vegas, NV 89107
(702)822-7700
https://www.springspreserve.org

More Las Vegas, Nevada

The best thing about Las Vegas is the desert around it. By going a little way outside of the city you can be in the middle of the desert where you won't see a single person, building or anything from the human race...just desert plants, rocks and animals to explore.

Aliante Nature Discovery Park aka Dinosaur Park

Dinosaur Park in Las Vegas Nevada is a prehistoric playground paradise! Not only is there a dinosaur sculpture to climb around, there are little cement dinosaur eggs that small people can crawl into and look like a newly-hatched dinosaur that is not ready to face the world. A climbing tower is there that has five stories and tube slides going from the top all the way to the bottom. There is a little fountain in a man-made pond that has live turtles in it and a fake alligator head that goes around in circles. There is also a large sand pit that has loads of room for digging up fossils.

Aliante Nature Discovery Park
Address: 2600 Nature Park Dr, N. Las Vegas, NV 89084
(866)874-6393

Red Rock Canyon National Conservation Area

Red Rock Canyon was selected to be the first National Conservation area in the state. This gem of a park is just 17 miles west of Las Vegas, NV. It is a favorite spot for rock climbers from all over the world who come to scale the steep rock cliffs.

It is fun to drive along the road that circles through the park. When you see dots of bright colors on the rock walls, you suddenly realize that it's a person scaling the sheer drop! There are all kinds of cactus and desert scenes to see along the way. The visitor center is one of the best I have ever experienced. It has both outdoor and indoor exhibits with lots of hands-on information. They also have small vehicles that you can rent (if you have a driver's license) that look like little go carts. It is definitely worth stopping in for a leisurely drive if you're in the Las Vegas area. You might just see wild donkeys on the road out there.

Red Rock Canyon National Conservation Area
3205 State Route 159, Las Vegas, NV 89161
http://www.redrockcanyonlv.org

Death Valley National Park
If you like to be close to the center of the earth, this is a good place to visit as it has the lowest point in the country at 282 feet below sea level. The best time to visit Death Valley is in the winter when the desert isn't so hot. Watch out though, because there are extreme temperature changes out here. It is super hot during the day but very cold at night. If you think the desert is a boring place to go, wait until you see the colors of the ridges...they are absolutely stunning. If you decide to stay and camp, you will have a view of the night sky that is unforgettable. At the visitor center, they have

a choice of Junior Ranger programs so you can decide whether to do the paleontology or regular program. I chose the paleontology one because it has pictures of dinosaurs on the badge.

Death Valley National Park
328 Greenland Blvd. Death Valley, CA 92328
(760)786-3280
http://www.nps.gov/deva

Devils Hole National Wildlife Refuge
Not far from Death Valley, but considered a detached section of it is Devils Hole. Just over the state line in Nevada, Devils Hole is a deep cavern in the ground with fresh water that has a unique species of fish.

If you look closely, you can see these endemic fish, which you will find no place else on earth. They are a bright shade of ocean blue with little specks of green lines on the sides of them. There is a raised walkway that brings you past many natural sights. Ranger programs are offered here with hikes available to the public.

Joshua Tree National Park

This national park right in southern California is really different from other deserts that are nearby. The Joshua Trees look like they are from another planet! The biggest one in the park is 40 feet high. Did you know that these are not like regular trees in another way? They don't have annual rings that grow on most trees. They are actually part of the yucca family.

I really like the desert because you can be out there and not see anyone for miles. You can also imagine what it would have been like for the settlers who passed through and saw these weird-looking trees. (Did you know that cactus can hold water inside? If you get stuck in the middle of the desert you can cut any kind with a knife and drink the water from the plant!) There are really cool trails here, including a big rock formation that looks like a skull. You may want to visit when it's cool out, because it really gets hot here.

Joshua Tree National Park
74485 National Park Dr, Twentynine Palms, CA 92277
(760) 367-6392
http://www.nps.gov/jotr

THE NORTHWEST

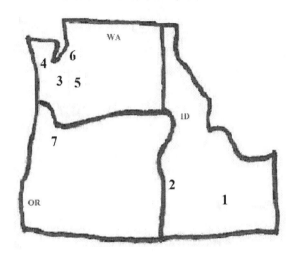

1. Craters of the Moon National Monument
2. World Center for Birds of Prey
3. Northwest Trek
4. The Quinault Rain Forest
5. Mt. Rainier National Park
6. Seattle, WA
7. Portland, OR

Really big trees are found in the Northwest.

THE NORTHWEST

Washington and Oregon have much to offer in the way of lush and gorgeous scenery. The western sides of the state have extremely rocky ocean beaches with incredibly large and exotic trees to see. As you go inland just a little ways, you will find that all the coastal rain brings springtime flowers growing all over! You can drive past large fields of flowers and mountain views that sparkle. The eastern parts of the states have more sun and snow but still many trees to see. Idaho has lovely waterfalls, streams and deep woods with natural wonders to explore. Imagine what this must have been like before Lewis and Clark came through!

Craters of the Moon National Monument

Imagine a lunar surface in which all you can see around you are mounds of black rocks and pebbles. This is my best description of Craters of the Moon National Park. The black rock is from lava flows that started 15,000 years ago (the last one was 2,000 years ago). This field of cooled lava is over 618 square miles across! There is much to look at, including a fascinating interpretive trail that points out the surrounding volcanoes in the area. I remember camping there with a really good friend and riding bikes with her and seeing all these bats flying around as the sun was setting. At the campground, the rangers offer an educational program in the nearby outdoor auditorium. At night, the stars were astonishing since there were no lights around the campground. I remember learning that we actually camped on one of the volcanoes and I said "what!?!" There is a lava tunnel that has cooled in such a way that you are able to walk through it. This is a very exciting park to visit and I would recommend it for all ages.

Craters of the Moon National Monument
400 W. F Street, Shoshone, ID 83352
(208) 527-1335
http://www.nps.gov/crmo/contacts.htm

World Center for Birds of Prey
If you really like birds of prey this is the place to go.

There is so much to see here that we went two days in a row so we could visit the magnificent Harpy Eagle again and tour the falconry museum. When I first went there, I was horrified by this bird from South America. Then I learned that it eats sloths and monkeys. What kind of bird goes after sloths and monkeys?! A really cool thing about them is that they have talons that are longer than a bear's claws! Later, I saw a documentary about Harpy Eagles that showed the only way the researchers could get a camera in the nest of a mated pair was to wear police riot gear and body armor for protection from the birds.

The falconry museum is all about the history of falconry through the ages. It has life size dioramas of people with falcons and they have hundreds of years' worth of information on birds of prey. When we were there, we actually walked into one of the life-sized dioramas in the museum, sat down amongst the wax figures and listened to the speakers in the tent. It was just like being there! Definitely a cool place to visit.

World Center for Birds of Prey
5668 W Flying Hawk Lane, Boise, ID 83709
(208)362-8687
http://www.peregrinefund.org/

Northwest Trek

This wildlife preserve has many animals from the Northwest. Some are kept in a fairly wide-open space. There is a bus-type of tram that takes you around the property to see wild animals in a large enclosure. It is so large, in fact, that you don't realize there is a fence keeping the animals from leaving. There are bison, elk, moose, and other large creatures to be viewed along with many birds. From the tram, you can take pictures and safely observe the animals that are there; it is really fun. There are also predators that are kept in separate areas and live in different pens. Some of them are: cats such as bob cats, mountain lions, bears and wolves. Some of the animals are being rehabilitated, and many volunteers help out to provide a good quality of life to the animals. There are large birds of prey such as eagles and different types of owls. Part of it seems like a zoo but it is nice to see some of the animals living in a large space out where the tram goes. There are areas for picnics and lots of trails to walk.

Northwest Trek
11610 Trek Dr E, Eatonville, WA 98328
(360)832-6117
http://www.nwtrek.org

The Quinault Rain Forest

The Quinault Rain Forest is the only temperate rain forest in North America. It is located on part of the Olympic National Park in Washington state. There used to be lots of primeval temperate rain forests in the world but now they are mostly only found in protected areas in Washington, southern Australia, New Zealand and Chile.

Some of the largest trees in the world are found in this area. The rain forest is just what it sounds like...it's very wet! There are huge, brightly-colored slugs nearby and I learned all about nurse logs. The trail takes you up past many lush, green plants and berry bushes. There are waterfalls and a rushing river below. If you are lucky, you can see some birds or an otter playing nearby.

Although this trail is fairly short, there are scenic lakes and campgrounds in the area where you can spend a night or stop for a picnic lunch. Make sure you are prepared for wet weather, no matter what time of year you go.

Olympic National Park Visitor Center
3002 Mt. Angeles Rd, Port Angeles, WA 98362
(360) 565-3130
http://www.nps.gov/olym

Mt. Rainier National Park
On a clear day, the drive up to the top of Mt. Rainier is a spectacular trip to make. Not only will you find snow all year round, the road has many places to stop and enjoy the views.

Did you know that Mt. Rainier is an active volcano

that could go off at any time? It also is the most glaciated mountain in the lower 48 states and generates six large rivers. If you decide to stop along the way, you can follow a trail that will take you over a fast, rushing river.

Wherever you look, it seems like the natural habitat is very busy and large in life. The trees reach way up into the sky and the river flows hard and fast. Dress warm, even in the summer! Once you get to the top of the mountain you can ski, year round. There is also an educational visitor center where you can participate in the Jr. Ranger Program.

Mount Rainier National Park
55210 238th Avenue East Ashford, WA 98304
(360)569-2211
http://www.nps.gov/mora/contacts.htm

Seattle

The city of Seattle offers a wealth of interesting sights to explore. It is spread out across the many scenic hills and waterways. You can ride a monorail through part of the city and enjoy Seattle's variety of parks and lakes. We have spent delightful afternoons walking along the piers and going to delicious restaurants. Keep your raincoats handy.

One of the best places to visit in Seattle is the fish ladder at the Ballard Locks. The entrance along the side of the lock lets you walk up a stairway and you can look through many windows and see salmon of all sizes going up underwater steps. It's fascinating to watch them move along and rest between levels. They also have a large room with a glass wall so you can see local sea creatures underwater. In another area, they have interactive displays to learn about Seattle's history, the salmon cycle and how a lock works. If you're lucky, you might get to see a boat go through the lock.

Ballard Locks
3015 NW 54th St, Seattle, WA 98107

(206) 783-7059
http://www.nws.usace.army.mil/Missions/Civil-Works/Locks-and-Dams/Chittenden-Locks/

Portland

Portland is a delightful city that has loads of specialty shops, bookstores and restaurants. They have lovely fountains around the city to tour, which can be particularly fun on a warm day. We like to visit the farmer's market, the marinas and see the city...especially around the holidays when the town looks so pretty.

My favorite place to visit in Portland is the Oregon Museum of Science and Industry (OMSI). They have an actual submarine parked in the water at the museum dock that you can go down into! I enjoyed walking around inside of it and seeing the periscope and how so many people lived every day in such a small space. For me, the best part was the torpedo room because it was cool to see what submarines use to destroy ships. If you plan ahead, you can even spend a night on the sub!

Oregon Museum of Science and Industry
1945 SE Water Ave., Portland, OR 97214
(503) 797-4000
http://www.omsi.edu

Wild Herb Camp in New England

4. SOCIALIZATION

We spend the first year of a child's life teaching it to walk and talk and the rest of its life to shut up and sit down. There's something wrong there. –
Neil deGrasse Tyson

The one question that people always ask is whether I have friends and meet with other kids on my travels. You bet! It isn't hard to make friends because there are homeschooling groups everywhere. On a regular basis, I meet people from all over.

We have found that finding kids to spend time with is simply not an issue. When it looks like we will stay in an area for a little while, we sign up for local activities where Rockett can get together with peers. Roadschooling has helped him to be outgoing and gifted at making new friends to keep in touch with. If local activities listed do not catch Rockett's attention, I have often started up meetings of different events on my own, such as Nerf Wars, Homeschool Sports, Swimming Lessons, Marine Science, Martial Arts, Lego events, Improvisation and Art classes. I can often receive discounts from venues when arranging them for homeschoolers. When we move on, we set up Skype video calls so that Rockett can continue "meeting" with his friends wherever they live. Doing so can also provide his friends with the opportunity to meet each other on line for group Skype meetings.

There are big advantages to meeting new people regularly. When we first began this adventure, a few folks were concerned that Rockett would struggle making new friends all the time, as children who move a lot often encounter when starting at a school in their new location. The difference is the setting; if school classmates are hard to befriend, the child is forced to have to deal with an uncomfortable situation for the remainder of the day, if not the rest of the year. Roadschooling, however, has more built-in flexibility; the child is not required to stay in a socially awkward environment. In our experience, it is much easier to learn to deal with difficult people in spurts with breaks and less time in a bad situation makes it less likely for antisocial habits to develop.[2]

Having an attentive adult to guide a child through challenging situations can help them to learn social skills faster. For example, we spent several months

---

[2] http://www.apa.org/helpcenter/resist-violence.aspx

in Las Vegas when Rockett was seven. The playgrounds there are fabulous! Filled with artistic structures of dinosaurs, Old West scenes and intricate water parks, there was so much fun to be had. The only problem was that there was often an unpleasant social climate among the local neighborhood kids who were reluctant to play with a newcomer, namely Rockett. Longing to enjoy their company, he would at first, feel very hurt when the other kids refused his requests to play. I silently witnessed this repeated scenario from a park bench. At first, when kids left him out he would feel bad and withdraw into himself. I pulled him aside and we talked about what was going on and came up with a plan. The next time it happened, he would put up an imaginary Impenetrable Shield of Playfulness (ISP), in which he would insist upon having fun by himself, no matter what the other kids did. He followed through with the plan. Eventually, most of the kids found his ISP attitude irresistible and decided to play with him. Years later, Rockett continues to use that skill when needed.

When Rockett became a tween, I signed up for a volunteer position at a primitive campground where I was the camp host to private groups of campers. A group of 15 to 30 campers would arrive together and spend usually three to five days at our campground. Often, classes of seventh or eighth graders camped and the teachers graciously invited Rockett along on their beach studies, tours and adventures. I mentioned to him that this was a golden opportunity to try out different personalities as he would be unlikely to see most of those kids again. He not only got the chance to socialize with kids in a school climate for several days at a time, he enjoyed having the freedom to experiment with socialization in a way that most children are limited to summer camp to explore.

Community service provides a unique opportunity to learn how the world works, to gather skills and to mingle with people of all ages.

It's not just kids that I make friends with. I have met the most remarkable adults, ever! I have learned about all kinds of cool things, like skydiving and preserving forests. I am so lucky to keep in touch with interesting grownups.

Rockett now has friends who are park rangers, business owners, volunteers and environmental enthusiasts. He is fortunate to have several mentors whom he can reach out to talk to and visit.

5. SINGLE-PARENT FAMILY LIFE ON THE ROAD

OUR MODE OF TRAVEL

There are many vehicle selections that will work for folks who decide to live on the road. Although I might have chosen to travel in a large recreational vehicle (RV), I decided on a small camper van as there are only two of us and space is much less of a premium to us than travel. A small RV has the advantage of being easy to get around in and can be parked almost anywhere (height limitations withstanding), that can save a lot on parking costs. Our camper van is twenty feet long, just over ten feet tall and is much like a tiny house[3] - only better because it is mobile. It is small, but very comfortable as it is tall enough to easily move around inside and has almost everything we need: a fridge, sink, stove, lots of storage and enough space to sleep three people. It also has a generator, solar panel, three batteries and both fresh and gray-water (dish water) tanks so we are

---

[3] https://en.wikipedia.org/wiki/Tiny_house_movement

not limited to spending nights in campgrounds or RV parks. I chose not to have a potty as I prefer to avoid the trouble of having to empty a black water (sewage) tank. We also have a bike rack for our bicycles. Finally, because I'm in a camper van and I don't have to pull a trailer, if in the middle of the night something happens and I want to leave the area, I can simply climb into the driver's seat and head down the road without having to unlock any doors. Rockett has a different experience of roadschooling as he sees the journey from the passenger seat.

When we are traveling a lot, I spend lots of time sitting. That's when I do my studying. When that's done, I look out the window, read, play with Legos and listen to audiobooks. The great thing about audio books is that you can get the ones that go with the type of trip that you are taking. For example, we did a trip along the wagon trail and my mom and I listened to The Little House on the Prairie books by Laura Ingalls Wilder along with some books about Native Americans. My mom always looks ahead for interesting places to stop along the way.

One of the reasons I wanted to take this adventure was to spend more time in nature, so I purposely have not invested in a satellite dish for the camper. I prefer to stay in locations that are as wire-free as possible so we can enjoy the natural world around us. However, since I do use a fair amount of audio and video for homeschooling and work, it is nice to have the option of electronic resources. When we are tired of traveling and need to get out of the camper for a while but the weather isn't so great, libraries are a favorite place to stop. One library had a children's section with computers that had the video game *Minecraft*[4] on them so the kids could play in unison. That was a real treat for Rockett, so we stayed in the area for a few days and he spent several afternoons playing with the local kids while I worked on my laptop at a nearby table. Libraries are often fun to explore. Some will let you borrow books by charging a small amount for a temporary card. If you cannot borrow a book, there are usually books for sale. Many people access ebooks and audiobooks through the internet or their home libraries. We download them on our cell phone, as well.

I tend to avoid stopping at malls or shopping centers as it is too tempting to spend money on unnecessary items. If we stay at a campground, most offer activities, sports, DVD rentals and, in some locales, classes for a small fee. We often stop for mealtimes at parks and wildlife viewing areas where we can get out and explore. Some of our best times are spent following bird-watching signs that take us down dirt roads to delightfully unexpected places.

HOW WE HOMESCHOOL

Do not train a child to learn by force or harshness; but direct them to it by what amuses their minds, so that you may be better able to discover with accuracy the peculiar bent of the genius of each. – Plato

Every homeschooling family has different philosophies and practices. Homeschooling for us is loosely based on workbooks that cover the basics:

---

[4] Mi*necraft* is a popular video game in which you can build structures in different locations in the program, sort of like Legos in a video format.

math, science, language arts, history and writing skills. These are the ones Rockett slowly works through before being tested each spring or summer, whenever I feel he is ready. He also reads and listens to books or watches videos on a diverse range of subjects as well as various art, athletic and music projects. I will usually find as many ways to incorporate a particular topic as I can find. For example, when he was learning about electricity, we picked up books and videos on Nicola Tesla and Thomas Edison, went to a science museum to explore exhibits on lightning, got him a scholarship to a robotics class and found an electronics kit for him to experiment with. These are some homeschooling techniques that usually work well for us:

- Organizing subjects around Rockett's current interests. For example, when he was heavily into dinosaurs, he learned dinosaur math, dinosaur writing, dinosaur science, etc.
- Reading books for small children in Spanish and practicing during real-life events.
- Never insisting that he study a topic he is not in the mood for. For example, if his brain isn't up for math, we might play cards or read a book instead.
  It is always beneficial to have a mentor who takes an interest in learning skills. Rockett is fortunate to have an online mentor from Abrome. They meet on line a few times a month and his mentor is fabulous at keeping Rockett on track to learn what interests him most. Abrome is a mentor program that offers individual attention to teens who are independent learners. See: www.abrome.com
- Finding books, DVDs and online information about subjects that Rockett is interested in learning.
- Flash cards work well for him. Whether they are for vocabulary, spelling or math, they can be turned into a fun game, especially when Mom doesn't know all the answers. Sometimes we play them backwards, doing answers first and guessing the

opposite side. For example, listing the capital first instead of the state.

- Picking up books and DVDs about a myriad of subjects to introduce new concepts and experiences.
- Using objects around us to do math. For example, using shells on a beach for division, calculating map mileage, observing temperatures, counting change in stores, starting his own retail business and using anything hands on to explain how a process works.
- Finding local and online groups of people who have similar interests.

Here are some learning methods that have NOT worked for us in homeschooling:

- Lengthy times sitting and filling out workbooks or doing anything not fun.
- Insisting Rockett study a specific topic when he is not in the mood. For example, we may switch it from math to reading or art, depending on what feels right.
- Attending classes that require the kids to sit for long periods of time without interaction.
- Watching or reading anything boring.

Memorial after the Boston Marathon bombing

The rest of what Rockett learns is all around us. Whether volunteering in a permaculture garden or visiting a specific park, we research each topic to learn more. For instance, shortly after he had studied President Franklin Delano Roosevelt and his Works Progress Administration, Rockett and I visited a national historic site where the Civilian Conservation Corps had assembled some of the roads and buildings. He immediately recognized both how and when the lodgings and roadways were constructed. This is just one way we've learned history "in action."

Fourth of July in the South

Social Studies is always a great subject to cover while traveling. Among other societal issues, Rockett has learned about discrimination. We have visited the Holocaust Museum in Washington D.C. and walked through plantations in the south. He has learned about The Trail of Tears, the internment camps during World War II and the indentured servitude of the Irish. In addition, he learns about everyday discrimination around him when he notices things such as Confederate flags, hears news about LGBT issues and notices gender discrimination at nature programs offered at museums, national parks and the like where a ranger or instructor refers to all animals as "He." We talk about how referring to all creatures as being male is scientifically incorrect and teaches children that it is proper to assign priority to males of all species across the board. We also discuss when it is appropriate to speak up about issues and when it is not safe to do so.

MEALTIME

There comes a moment on a journey when something
sweet, something irresistible and charming as wine
raised to thirsty lips, wells up in the traveler's being. –
Patrick MacGill

When it comes to food, every family has their favorite meals and snacks. Since we are vegan and gluten-free, our meal planning can be a challenge, especially when we're on the road. I like to stock up on specialty items such as seaweed, tamari sauce, miso paste, all kinds of canned or dried beans, whole grain pastas, rice and fresh fruits and veggies. Wherever we go, we are always looking for local specialties to liven up our meals.

We like snacks as much as anyone else! I don't have an oven, but my quick roll recipe (a mixture of garbanzo bean flour, almond flour and tapioca along with a bit of oil and seasonings) can be made on the stovetop in my cast iron skillet. (I've also figured out how to make brownies, cookies and sweet rolls in that cast iron skillet!) Aside from chips, we also came up with a bunch of other treats that travel well so we don't need to stop at restaurants.

The thing about traveling is that not just any food is good for a moving vehicle. From personal experience, bananas are the worst travel food ever! They bruise easily and are no good after a few days. If you are a picky eater (like me) you will hate them. The best travel food is salad because it can stay fresh, doesn't get bruised easily and makes for a fast and easy meal.

On a long trip, it can be really satisfying to pull into a scenic rest area for a meal and get out of the camper for a bit. It's like having a picnic every day. When short on time, there are some delicious instant soups that cook up quickly. If I know I have a long trip ahead of me, I will often make some rolls to snack on while driving. Hummus, refried beans, chips, guacamole, tofu slices, chopped veggies and condiments go far for a swift and nutritious meal with easy clean up. Most of our staples can be found at any grocery store. Others, like tofu, can require some purchasing ahead of time, depending on what part of the country is being traveled. We always make a point to enjoy local specialties along the road. Whether picking up salsa in New Mexico, black eyed peas in Georgia or stopping at farm stands on back roads, the subject of food is rich with possibilities for learning about different cultures, topography and agriculture.

OUR TRAVEL PLANS

When we first began roadschooling full time, we followed no set schedule and went wherever the next experience led us. This is a delightful way to approach traveling. One fall, we decided to head back to the Northwest to spend the winter with friends. We meandered our way out west from Vermont and planned to stop in Boise to investigate a Bird Sanctuary there. Once we arrived, we were so enthralled with their birds that we decided to find a local RV park to spend the night and go back to see them again the next day. It turned out that a large snow storm came over the mountains that night. A few days later, I asked the local RV park owner when he expected the mountain roads to clear of snow so we could continue on our journey north. He looked at me and said,

"March?" I thought he was kidding but he wasn't; one extra day had made all the difference! I got a call that night from a friend who was living and working in Las Vegas at the time. When I told her about what had happened, she suggested, "Come on down and spend the winter here." I spoke to Rockett about it and he liked the idea, so we spent a winter in the Southwest exploring deserts. We have had many unforgettable experiences just seeing where things take us.

Last year, I decided to look into volunteer positions available to RVers. I wanted Rockett to have some more opportunities for learning from professionals. This introduced us to more novel experiences in different parts of the country. Our first volunteer position was at one of the US Army Corps of Engineers Visitor Centers. Four days a week, while our camper was parked in the RV area reserved for volunteers, we assisted in the visitor center assisting the public as they learned about the area. Rockett was very proud in his volunteer shirt and badge and he liked to hand out pamphlets and put on the educational film that visitors watched. We enjoyed that for several weeks and then moved on to another state to take a campground host position, this time at a state park. Different parks offer different opportunities to explore and most are usually willing to accommodate their volunteers' schedules; therefore, it's often possible to take excursions for short or long periods of time.

After we were on the road in the camper van for about a year, I decided to get my car out of storage and keep it with us. It's convenient to have for running errands and because it is small, it tows easily behind the camper van. On some of our trips, we leave the camper van parked in a safe place and travel by car with our tent and camping supplies. Our mode of travel mostly depends on the season, the price of fuel and the kind of adventure we have in mind. It is nice to have an option.

THE SINGLE-PARENT FACTOR

There is no school equal to a decent home and no teacher equal to a virtuous parent. – Mahatma Gandhi

There are many advantages to RV living as a single parent. Because there are just two of us, we fit comfortably in a small space. If there were another person along we might need a larger vehicle. A small family has the benefit of a smaller number of belongings to keep up with and fewer people whose needs require attending. Having a modest-sized dwelling makes it so there is less space to clean. When I need to run out for groceries or anything else, our home is never far away, so errands are completed faster.

As you might imagine, being a homeschooling single-parent can be very demanding. It requires a juggling act of the big three time challenges: earning a living, homeschooling and life maintenance. Life maintenance includes all the things that need doing besides the first two, such as cooking, cleaning, grocery shopping, laundry, parent-child playtime, social contacts, doctor visits, bill-paying, vehicle maintenance, and finding time for oneself. As with any family, the love and caring from extended family and friends can make a big difference. Although being on the road can limit the ability to leave my son at a friend's house while I take care of errands or business, there is the advantage of not needing much child care.

Friends have asked me how I get my own time each day. Starting when Rockett was about three, at the end of the day I explained to him that it was "adult time," which meant that this was when mom did her grown up things such as reading quietly to herself, watching a show that she enjoyed or talking on the phone while he was in bed. He could be in the same room and see what I was up to, but it was clear that it was time for me to mostly focus on other things. Maintaining a balance that keeps everyone's needs met is always a constructive goal that changes with the ages and stages for each of us.

I would find roadschooling as a single parent difficult to do with a child much younger than about six, depending on the child, of course. Although travel with kids of any age is beneficial because it opens them up to new experiences, I waited for Rockett to be old enough to remember his adventures and be able to tolerate sitting for long periods of time during lengthy trips. When we first headed out, he wasn't too interested in looking at the scenery outside the window. As he got older and could comprehend the concept of maps a bit better, the scenery became more interesting to him. By the time he was ten, he had been to 44 states and developed a keen interest in seeing the rest. We have found a rhythm on the road that works for both of us.

No matter what your current marital or family situation, what makes the best travels possible is a solid connection to loved ones. Not only do we have our special folks who keep track of where we are through regular phone calls, we have a good friend whom I can call for trusted advice whenever I have a problem with one of my vehicles. We also have loved ones who we chat with regularly to keep all of us connected. If it were not for these people, we would not be able to be on this journey.

SOME MEMORABLE ROADSCHOOLING MOMENTS

There are a myriad of unique experiences that Rockett and I will never forget. It is difficult for us to choose the best ones! Some happen whenever we have had any vehicle problems on a trip; it seems that the kindest people come out of nowhere to give us a hand. We have wonderful memories of folks who were helpful to us when we needed it the most. Here are some of our most savored moments:

- While driving through Mt. Zion National Park in Utah, we were about to go through a tunnel in a rock mound when we looked up to see a pair of mountain goats above us. They were so spectacular! (See photo.)
- At one point, we were in Florida for several weeks. Our RV parking space was within 50 feet of a bunch of trees where wild panthers gathered each night. They would sit there and wait to go chase the cattle kept in a paddock across the street from us. We often walked past the large panthers and one

night, noticed one of their babies watching us walk past.

- Driving across Interstate 90 one summer evening, we stopped in upstate New York to have dinner at a rest area. As the sun began to set, a bunch of fireflies danced around our camper van. It was magical to see them flicker in the waning light.

- On one trip, our quest was to hear the mating calls of alligators. We visited several swamps and waterways, asking the local experts where we could go to hear the alligators make their calls. Most of them told us that it was too early in the season and our hearts sank. Then, one ranger suggested that we might get lucky in the morning, so we got up at dawn the following day and headed out into the Okefenokee Swamp in a canoe with high hopes. The swamp air was still and filled with mist rising above the black water. Suddenly, we heard a long, low growl that seemed to reverberate across the top of the placid water. That was it!!! We both looked at each other and smiled with glee. It sounded so prehistoric, it was truly a thrill.

- Have you ever gone out in an area in the dark that has a lot of insects? If you go outside at night with a good flashlight and hold it up to your eye level, you will see a ton of green spider eyes staring back at you. The first time I did this, I couldn't believe how many spiders were watching me. If you are afraid of spiders, don't do it!

- Death Valley National Park in California is an exceptional place to visit in the daytime. We saw so many lovely colors as we drove around and looked at the ground below our feet and the mountains along the horizon. What was even more surprising was the view from the campground at night of the fullest sky of stars we had ever seen!

- Sitting at the picnic table in our quiet campsite in central Florida one afternoon, we suddenly heard a long, low and strong hum of bees. We looked up to see a mass of 20,000 to 40,000 bumble bees and perhaps killer bees (or so we were told later) swarm into the tree above our camper van. A ranger came over and whispered for us to quietly get into the camper van, make sure all vents and windows were closed then start it up and slowly drive out of the campsite making as little noise or sudden moves as possible. It reminded me of a scene in *The Birds*. Luckily, we got out of there without disturbing them while they built a nest in the trees.
- We were swimming in a Florida cove on the Atlantic Ocean when a large manatee entered and swam with us. Since they are herbivores and peaceful creatures, we were delighted that he or she chose to swim near us.
- Having climbed to the top of a 750 foot tall sand dune at Great Sand Dunes National Park in Colorado, we stopped to rest and take in the view of the surrounding mountains. When we looked down, we discovered cute little beetles crawling in the sand next to us.
- We woke up one morning to find three wild ponies grazing at our campsite on Assateague Island, Maryland. We sat quietly and watched them sniff our fireplace and graze in our campsite until they wandered off.
- We were recently visiting good friends where Rockett was playing *Minecraft* with the kids. At one point, the kids were constructing houses and they noticed that Rockett's character kept disappearing in the game to explore the area instead of building like they were. The kids asked why he didn't want to build a house and their father responded, "Because he's a nomad."

- I stopped to buy supplies at a Trader Joe's grocery store in Jacksonville, Florida. It was a very stormy day and we were soaking wet. Still drenched from the downpour outside, I pushed my full cart up to a register where the cashier asked if I was having a stressful day. I looked at Rockett and said, "I guess it's been a bit challenging with the rain." After I paid for the groceries, the cashier said "Wait a minute, please" then dashed off and returned with a bouquet of flowers for me and she said "This is for you." I was deeply touched.

We have been roadschooling for some time now and we both love it. Each day is a new adventure! Sometimes people at the parks will be so kind to Rockett. The rangers will give him special opportunities to spend time with animals or offer him things like flashlights and camping knives...people can be so wonderful. Between the sights we see and the special people and creatures we run across, these moments will be cherished for a long time. Hopefully, you will have many favorite roadschooling memories of your own to share.

6. PLANNING YOUR ROADSCHOOLING BUDGET

There's a book that tells you where you should go on your vacation. It's called your checkbook. –
Author Unknown

Whether you wish to roadschool for a short or long time, you will want to plan ahead and see which adventures and modes of travel are likely to work best for your family. There are many details involved with roadschooling that need consideration. Here are some tools that I have picked up over the years that have helped to assure some great adventures at low cost.

THE COST OF LIVING ON THE ROAD

The good news about roadschooling is that it reduces the biggest bill for most families. United States households spend from one third to one half of their income on housing. This includes utilities such as gas, electric, trash and water. Once on the road, your housing costs can be greatly reduced. So much so, that some people opt to live in a recreational vehicle in order to save money to purchase a house!

Your roadschooling costs will depend upon several variables including the cost and size of your vehicle, maintenance, insurance coverage, where you park and fuel consumption. A large family will require a larger vehicle that will be heavier due to hauling more bodies and belongings than a smaller family. You can decide to purchase a new or used vehicle and select the kind of setup that meets your needs. Some families prefer to include a separate car or truck to make local trips without having to bring their RV everywhere. As you read about the following topics, you will learn a bit how to help you to calculate and manage your budget.

EMPLOYMENT

There are numerous types of employment that can be done while on the road. I have met online teachers, attorneys, salespeople, writers, customer service specialists, contract medical professionals, maintenance technicians, crafters and artists. There are also temporary jobs available in RV parks and campgrounds, and even Amazon has a program offered in several states where people can live and work seasonally in their RV (see below). Many people find that their income is reduced while working on the road but again, the housing cost is lower so that is worth taking into consideration. Below are some online sites that offer job listings for RV owners that you can sign up to receive regular emails:

http://www.coolworks.com/jobs-with-rv-spaces/
http://www.work-for-rvers-and-campers.com/
http://www.roadworking.com/rver-jobs.html
https://www.workamper.com/
*http://www.amazonfulfillmentcareers.com/opport
unities/camper-force/*

SELECTING A VEHICLE

It is possible to roadschool in a car or a van while sleeping in a tent, but unless you are a seasoned camper, you will find it limits you to warmer weather and lacks the conveniences of already having a dry place to cook, wash dishes, etc. The good news about recreational vehicles is that purchasing one is different from buying a car; you can get much longer loan terms on new and almost-new RVs, often ranging from 8 to 20 years, making low monthly payments possible - some under $200 a month. You can spend a lot of time looking over recreational vehicle options for roadschooling. Hopefully, this will help you to narrow down your search.

Basically, there are two different types of RVs: ones that you pull and ones that you drive. The ones that you pull - which include travel trailers, tent trailers and fifth wheels – tend to cost less, since they do not have a motor. An advantage to this type of RV is that it will provide you a vehicle that you can drive separately without hauling your RV everywhere with you. RVs that have a motor in them tend to be more expensive. In addition, unless you pull a car behind you or have a motorcycle or bike rack, your home will be your only transportation.

Some recreational vehicles are pulled with a truck or SUV

Other recreational vehicles come with a motor to be driven as one unit[5]

As a general rule, the larger the vehicle, the more fuel it requires and more challenges for parking – daytime or overnight. When deciding what type of RV will be best for you, it is helpful to consider whether you plan on covering a lot of miles most of the time or if you plan to park in one location and use your tow vehicle to get around in, as one might use the pickup truck that hauls a trailer. More mileage means more fuel costs whereas less mileage can have parking fees be the biggest expense. But again, it all depends how you go about it: whether you are off the grid, in a campground or spending your nights in places where you volunteer or work in lieu of paying for your parking space.

Look long and hard at different kinds of setups before you decide which one to purchase. For more specifics, I suggest that you go to a recreational vehicle dealership and see what is out there. If you visit *www.gorving.com*, you can see photos, pricing and a comparison of RV possibilities. Be sure to take a vehicle

---

[5] A truck can have the slide-out camper removed; however it is not designed for living in without the vehicle to support it.

for a several days' test drive whenever possible so you can get a genuine feel for what it will be like over time. Lastly, just like buying a car, never buy a used vehicle without having a trusted mechanic go over it thoroughly previous to purchasing.

FINANCES

Banking can be fairly simple if you are up to date with your electronics. With my Android phone I can make deposits, pay bills and transfer funds. I get cash at supermarkets or banks that are in my network. I prefer to use a credit union as it is easy to find participating credit unions in any state to avoid paying ATM fees. I tend to use a credit card as it makes keeping track of my expenses easier and I get a percentage back from its usage. I do not advise using an ATM card for most things such as purchasing gas or dining at restaurants. Unless I have no other option, I only use an American Express credit card as they (so far) have managed to catch unauthorized charges on my card. (They were also great about sending a new card overnight to me while on the road.) Whatever card you take along with you, it is a good idea to let the bank know that you are traveling so that they will not be alarmed when they come across charges from different states.

When it comes to sticking to a budget, it can take a little while to figure out that this style of living is not a vacation. For example, we only go to amusement parks or dine out on special occasions. Some families find that spending more time out and about leads to spending more on items such as snacks and shopping. If you plan to eat at home in your RV, your food bill shouldn't change much from what it is now unless your refrigerator is much smaller than usual.

Buying in bulk offers better prices usually but living in a RV often does not afford the space for lots of food storage.

There are a few more expenses that need consideration such as mail services and homeschool requirements which can vary and are discussed later. You definitely want to make sure that you have enough cushion in your savings to cover any emergencies or unexpected maintenance issues.

DECIDING ON A HOME BASE

If you make the decision to roadschool for a lengthy period, you will want to settle on which state will be your home base. If you take the time to research different insurance and registration fees, you will find that it may be worth selecting a state other than the one you are currently living in now. You may choose to change your driver's license registration if you find it less expensive to purchase a vehicle in another state. To learn about different registration laws and their requirements for a RV, you can go to www.escapees.com or search the topic online. In addition, different states have their own homeschooling laws that need to be adhered to. You will want to have your children registered and follow that state's laws. Check www.hslda.org to learn more about each state's homeschool laws.

HOMESCHOOLING

Once you have decided which state will be your home base, you can then follow the guidelines to learn what to do in keeping within that state's educational requirements. Beyond that, whether you are a seasoned homeschooler or new to the process, homeschooling choices are unique to each family. Some families use online programs, some use workbooks and others unschool. I use library resources as much as possible to save on costs through downloading books online and also because we do not always have internet access.

It is important to keep items to a minimum when living on the road; however, I make room for art supplies, musical instruments and homeschooling books. At one point, we carried an electronic piano keyboard that tucked away nicely. I send my son's completed workbooks to be placed in storage and I have him tested each year at his grade level via exams that I order online and give to him myself. As with all homeschoolers, it is an excellent idea to keep any educational records you have for future reference.

VEHICLE INSURANCE/TOWING DISCOUNTS

Whether shopping for home, car, or health insurance, it is to your benefit to spend some time carefully reviewing exactly what kind of coverage you will need for the state your vehicle will be registered and for what type of usage. You will be asked the estimated mileage usage as well as the value of the vehicle. They also want to know if you will be living in your RV full or part time. I made the mistake of paying for too much insurance when I first started. I was talked into scary scenarios such as, if another child falls and gets hurt while on the camping space I had rented for the night. It wasn't until later that I realized the kids mostly are at the playground, not running around in a small parking area. Get lots of quotes and pay close attention to coverage amounts.

Some insurance companies offer a towing

option on their policy. Depending on the size of your vehicle, AAA might be a good option. They offer an annual membership that provides coverage for RV towing that isn't much more than what it costs for a car. I also like AAA because of the discount it provides when going to many entertainment venues including parks and hotels. Always keep in mind that recreational vehicles are a different animal than regular cars. Some RV clubs offer towing services but again, be a smart shopper and look closely at the prices and benefits.

PARKING YOUR RV

Finding a place to park can be a challenge, especially with large vehicles. When you are traveling along the highways there are usually truck stops and all night facilities available to pull into to spend a few hours or the night. Most Wal-Mart stores and Cracker Barrel restaurants offer free overnight parking for RVs but not everywhere. In many parts of Florida for example, the town ordinances do not permit it and it can be very startling to get a knock on the door by a police officer waking you up in the wee hours of the morning. Some townships will even hand you a fine!

Visiting cities and more populated areas is another story. For larger RVs, you will save yourself a lot of trouble if you do the research ahead of time when you plan to arrive in a specific location. The easiest way to learn about parking laws is to contact the local police department of the municipality you plan to visit and inquire about their ordinances. Some will permit on-street parking during the day but not overnight, while others will not allow any recreational vehicle parking at any time. With our small camper van, we are frequently able to find on-street parking with minimal restrictions because it only takes up one parking space.

Often, the local authorities can refer you to a campground or RV park in the area.

There are many different kinds of camp-grounds and RV parks across the country. Some are privately owned and others are run by a state, county or federal government. Most campgrounds and RV parks that provide full hook-ups can run anywhere from approximately $15 to over $60 per night. Parking closer to a large city tends to be higher than rural areas. Many businesses will offer a discounted rate for lengthier stays at their park. If you know ahead of time that you want to remain in an area for a while, you can save quite a bit on space rental as they will often offer a monthly rate that can be anywhere from a few hundred dollars per month on up, depending upon the location. Sometimes that will include utilities and sometimes not.

There are several phone apps available with listings for RV parks, campgrounds and even free overnight parking locations. You will find that many RV folks take advantage of free overnight parking on local and federal property run by some counties or the Bureau of Land Management. Usually, these have no services such as restrooms, water or electricity, but will permit a fully-contained vehicle (meaning you have your own power source, water supply, restroom and holding tanks) to park for sometimes weeks or more at no charge. This is often referred to as 'boon docking' or parking 'off-grid.'

Another option is to seek volunteer and/or pay positions at a campground or RV park. This usually involves working approximately 20 to 30 hours per week per adult in exchange for a space to park that includes utilities. Some parks will pay for extra hours worked. Most privately owned parks will require the same. Many people reserve their volunteer positions months or years in advance. State and federal parks will require a background check and references. Depending on where you wish to go, you can research volunteer openings for particular states on their state park websites. There are a number of websites where you can sign up for email notifications of open positions. For suggestions of listings, see the "Volunteer Organizations" section.

MAINTAINING YOUR VEHICLE

I once overheard a customer at a repair shop say he learned the hard way that RV stood for "Ruined Vacation." Keep in mind that your RV is not only your means of transportation but your home, so it needs appropriate attention. Carry a notebook in your vehicle to keep track of all repairs and maintenance receipts. This will also save you if you installed a part with a lifetime warrantee that happens to go bad. You may have maintenance coverage for your vehicle if it is new or nearly new in which case, you would be directed where to get it repaired. If you have an older vehicle, it can be unsettling not knowing where to go for reliable service.

My camper van is older and on more than one occasion I have found myself needing a good mechanic. At first, I made the mistake of going to one or two franchise shops that I figured I could count on for repairs. Big mistake! Even those quick lube shops are questionable. I might go to them to get an oil change where I can easily check to make sure that the oil was actually changed and at the right level, but I would never have them do anything more involved, such as flushing a transmission. I have repeatedly found that the best resource is to call a local Auto Zone (or similar parts supply store) and ask for a referral to someone in the area who is a trustworthy mechanic. I have found the finest service doing this! One mechanic had me meet him at his shop in Indiana early on a Sunday morning where he welded a small part on my engine and charged me very little for it. Another time, a shop for large trucks in Minnesota put in a part for me and charged me a very reasonable price. Except for tires, it has been my experience that whenever I take my camper to a franchise shop, I get overcharged and/or poor service. There are small repair shops for all kinds of RVs. Go by local word of mouth whenever you can. Before you get too far making any service appointments, make sure that you know the height of your vehicle and that it will fit in the mechanic's bay. Many shops do not have doors tall enough to service RVs.

TIRE SERVICE

It is extremely important to have good tires on your RV. I always figured that I would never need to drive through snow or ice as my plan was to stay away from cold weather. I was very glad to know that I had new all-weather tires on the camper when I suddenly found myself driving through a snowstorm in Colorado one day. Remember, this is your home and you want it to be on a super-solid foundation. Tire service is where I rely on franchise shops to handle my vehicle's needs, the advantage being that I can have my tires repaired, rotated and replaced without additional costs in most cases. I recently went back to a Discount Tire shop in the South as I had originally purchased mine from one in the Northwest. They gave me credit toward a new set by exchanging my tires and I was pleasantly surprised by the price. Always make sure to buy your tires at a company that has work bays tall enough to accommodate your RV.

GETTING YOUR MAIL

Although you can get most of your mail taken care of via the internet, including bill paying and balance statements, there are some items that need to come via snail mail such as: vehicle registration, insurance documents, driver's licenses, medical cards, absentee ballots, tax documents and credit cards. You may have a reliable friend or relative who doesn't mind handling your mail. I suggest finding a private mail service - not the United States Postal Service - to take care of any mail forwarding. There are many companies that will not only forward your mail, they will also open, scan and email copies of it for you and can help establish state residency for vehicle registration and insurance. For more information you can search online under "mail handling services for travelers/RVs."

MEDICAL

When it comes to medical issues, most of the people I know who live on the road either use the local providers that their network covers or they make regular trips to their favorite doctors and dentists. I have always kept a record of my child's medical visits, vaccinations and any pertinent information. That way, not only am I able to keep track of his health, I can also bring his medical records anywhere with me if needed. It is a good idea to keep one on file for everyone in the family. I have had several incidents where medical facilities were not able to access their records. It's a good idea to keep one for your pets, too, especially if you leave them in the care of someone else.

SAFETY

Keep an emergency contact card with information on it handy in your vehicle and on your person. Make sure you have a well-stocked first aid kit, emergency funds and people available in case you need them. I do not spend the night in rest areas unless they are well-lit AND clearly monitored by the local authorities throughout the night. If I need to stop to sleep for a few hours, I usually park in a well-lit area of an all night gas station or truck stop. If it is on a quiet road without much traffic, I will walk into the store to ask the attendant if it's okay for "my husband and me" to rest in the parking lot for a few hours before heading down the road again. If the station is located in a busy area, it can be noisy where people are coming in and out to get gas but if I am that tired, I will be able to sleep. If I cannot find that type of situation, I have a large dog bowl that I place outside by the door of our vehicle...with water. (We don't have a dog.)

I make a point of not carrying any kind of personal protection that can be considered illegal into any state or national park. The last thing I want is to be arrested for not following some state or federal laws. Instead, I carry a large can of wasp spray that remains within arm's reach. In the past, I took a course in Model Mugging (that I think every female should take) which taught me many useful skills. I also speak at great lengths with my son about noticing other people and trusting your instincts. We have some systems set up to find each other if we happen to lose track of one another and we are very careful to pay attention to where we each are and our surroundings. We had a very scary 15 minutes at one of the Smithsonian Museums in Washington DC last year when we agreed to meet in the photo gallery and it turned out that there were two of them. We learned the hard way that being specific with our communication is essential.

DOWNSIZING

It is hard to imagine moving from a full-sized home into a small RV. This is where an experimental pre-trip can be really helpful. Once you go on even a short trip, you will get a feel for how much you need to bring. If you decide to go on the road for a long-time, you may want to free yourself of many things that are easily replaced. The main idea is to think small and lightweight. I stored my Vitamix when a friend gave me a mini bullet blender. I brought my three favorite pots and pans for meals. I now have an eye for things like rakes that expand from the handle and folding storage boxes. I have been fortunate to have good friends who let me park my car and store some items at their homes. It can take a little time to decide what stays and what goes. The same goes for toys: it is best to bring toys that can be played with in a small space. Things like radio controlled cars will be a waste of space unless they are designed for outdoor use. Drones come with restrictions in certain areas so be sure to check with the park staff if your child plans to bring one out for play. All in all, it is best not to worry too much about forgetting something important. Like hiking, you are much better off to lean on the side of less than more. Whatever you wind up leaving behind and missing later can usually be purchased wherever you go.

WHAT TO BRING

*If you wish to travel far and fast, travel light. Take off
all your envies, jealousies, unforgiveness, selfishness
and fears. – Cesare Pavese*

When you live in a RV, you learn right away that
you cannot bring a lot of books or toys because of the
lack of space. I decided to bring these: my computer,
Legos, card games, clothing, art supplies, a journal and
a DVD player. The DVD player lets me listen to audio
books and watch DVD's without Wi-Fi access. If you
have a satellite dish set up for Wi-Fi and cell service,
you may not need a DVD player depending on where
you travel. We use one because we like to be off the
grid as much as possible and some libraries have DVDs
to loan. The computer is especially handy for keeping
in touch with friends through Skype play dates and it
makes it easy to do all kinds of things from learning
languages to creating videos and writing this book.

You will want to bring games. Card games are
fun and a great way to learn strategies and math. I
would bring clothes that are practical because there
are times that you need pants with lots of pockets
that you can take part of the legs off. You are
definitely going to want to have your bike and helmet
because there are some really fun biking trails and
many exciting places that you can get to faster by
riding a bike. You have no idea how many times it has
come in handy. We often stop at thrift stores to pick
up inexpensive games, books, toys, movies, clothing and
donate (or rotate) my things that I no longer need.

Some of the basics to bring include a well-stocked first aid kit and the minimum amount of lightweight dishes, cookware and table settings that you can get by with. Bring clothing that dries quickly and doesn't wrinkle easily. Bring some basic tools and lots of healthy snack foods. Do not forget to pack important records such as passports, birth certificates and copies of legal documents including a copy of your family being registered as homeschoolers. (It can be used to get discount coupons in certain stores and entertainment venues.) Depending on what type of vehicle you are traveling in, you may have a built-in stove or not. I carry both an electric plate and a butane stovetop. What we have found to be absolutely indispensable are baby wipes (where would we be without unscented wipes?), an emergency weather radio for when you are out of cell range, and if you plan to be gone for a long time, rechargeable batteries and a charger are very helpful.

PETS

We see a lot of seniors who travel with their pets, mostly small dogs. We have met a few who travel with a cat. You would be hard-pressed to find bigger animal lovers than us. I don't believe roadschooling is a good match for most pets because so much time is spent outside of the RV, and at places that usually do not allow pets. Educational travel is a much different lifestyle than touring seniors. Unless you have the type of RV in which you can leave the air conditioning running for long periods of time while you are away from the vehicle (or the heater, depending upon the climate), having a pet will definitely put restrictions on your activities and locations you wish to visit.

As you can imagine, not all animals travel well in

a vehicle either. It took some time for our older kitty to adjust to life in our camper van. We loved having her with us and she seemed mostly fine sleeping the day away in the camper but we definitely cut short several of our sightseeing events and sometimes skipped places altogether to make sure that she was comfortable. I cannot imagine leaving a dog (or more) alone all day inside (or tied outside) a vehicle while off exploring parks and museums.

Some campgrounds do not permit pets. If they do, you often are required to show proof of recent vaccinations. A good friend of mine would travel with her dogs and had a difficult time finding campgrounds that allowed larger dogs. People often complain about barking dogs that are left in vehicles in parking lots and tied up for long hours at campgrounds. Many ferries will not allow a pet on board unless it is a service animal. Our kitty passed of natural causes when she was 15. We now spend quality time visiting other people's pets. If you love your pets you will make sure that they are in a place where they can get lots of good attention, be comfortable and safe.

7. MEMBERSHIPS AND TRAVEL SAVERS

There are many kinds of services, clubs and organizations that can be cost-effective for your roadschool adventures. There are discounts for RVers as well as for homeschoolers and think about any memberships or employment discounts that you may be eligible to receive. Some large chain stores including Barnes and Noble and Jo-Ann Fabrics and Craft Stores will offer a discount card to you if you provide a document showing your family is registered to homeschool. Wherever you go, it is a good idea to ask what discounts are available especially when you are entering RV parks or buying items for homeschooling. There are several groups you can join to receive emails about upcoming trips, volunteer positions, and many more. Here are a few suggestions to help your budget on your adventures.

TRAVEL OFF-SEASON

One of the greatest advantages of roadschooling is being able to avoid the crowds and heavy traffic that summertime brings. When you travel during the school year, you are not only more likely to have shorter lines and plenty of openings at different venues, there is often the added benefit of off-season rates. Many campgrounds reduce their rates, along with hotels and airlines. If you plan to fly to a location and rent a vehicle to travel with from there, this might be your best bet to do it low-cost. Be aware that hours of operation are often reduced as well, so be careful to plan accordingly.

VEHICLE/TRAVEL CLUBS

For larger vehicles, there are club member-ships that can provide deep discounts at campgrounds across the country. Usually, the discounts only apply during the off season. This can be a great advantage if you plan to travel at that time. Otherwise, it might not be worth the cost of membership. These memberships are often connected to vehicle insurance, such as Good Sam. If it is, be a careful shopper and do not get talked into unnecessary coverage. There are also clubs you can join that own property around the country that you can buy into and stay at their locations for lengthy periods. It can be quite pricey and you can be limited by their locations, but it is one way to travel with more secure parking. Always inquire if a RV park is family-friendly as many parks and clubs are designed for seniors only.

If you already can use the towing service for your car or RV, being a AAA member often has the benefit of discounts at many locations, including amusement parks, nature centers, hotels, car rentals and even some RV parks. An advantage to this service is that it covers the driver, not just the vehicle so no matter what kind of car you are driving you are covered for a tow. Don't forget the savings offered if you ever lock the keys in your vehicle, need a jump or a tow or free maps. (Policies change periodically so do some fact-checking prior to signing up.)

www.Goodsamclub.com

www.passportamerica.com

https://escapees.com

www.aaa.com (This link will redirect you to a local office website.)

GROUPON, ETC.

If you know ahead of time what part of the country you plan to visit, you can sign up for online coupons for that area ahead of time. It is possible to narrow your preferred coupons to different categories such as travel or entertainment. You can also usually do a search for preferred venues. Many of the coupons can be purchased with an open period in case you don't arrive exactly the date selected. Sometimes your bank, credit union, local library or Costco will offer discounts for venues.

TOLLS

If you plan to travel east of the Mississippi, you will want to get an E-Z Pass for your windshield. An E-Z Pass is a small, rectangular device that is mounted with adhesive strips next to your rear view mirror. When passing over a bridge or toll road, the device is picked up electronically and it automatically withdraws money from your account. Having an E-Z Pass is very convenient as it saves you money, spares you from stopping for tolls or the worry of paying toll charges sent to you via license plate photos that become bills in the mail. Currently, the E-Z Pass will work in 16 eastern states. Florida, Georgia and South Carolina each have a separate toll system that uses a different transponder. Each state has their own website that explains how best to obtain a pass. For example, Virginia's E-Z Pass website explains how to order one by phone, fax or online to have it shipped to you to be used in any E-Z Pass state. See *http://www.ezpassva.com*.

NATIONAL PARKS PASS

If you plan to visit many locations in the National Park Service (NPS), you will want to purchase an $80 annual parks pass that will save you a LOT of money throughout the year. There are currently 408 parks in the NPS. Some have no entrance fee at all but the more popular ones can be as high as $30 per vehicle. The parks pass easily pays for itself if you have plans to visit even a handful of the popular parks. Passes are available at many national park service facilities or can be purchased on line at *http://www.nps.gov*.

HOMESCHOOL TRAVEL GROUPS

It is fun to join up with other home-schoolers to go on a new adventure. Some groups rally at places ahead of time for a fee and others plan entire trips to go on together. The Traveling Homeschoolers Group is one that plans fun trips to a wide variety of places, both in and outside of the United States. See: *http://www.travelinghomeschoolers.com/*

The only problem is that finding these kinds of groups can be tricky as most are closed. Your best bet is to research homeschool travel/trips online or via social media.

MUSEUM MEMBERSHIPS

If you plan to visit science museums, you will want to become a member of a museum that is part of the Association of Science-Technology Centers (ASTC). The ASTC has over 600 museums that are science-related in 50 countries where members can visit for no admission fee (with some restrictions, so call first). Over 300 are located in the United States. You can join by becoming a member of a participating museum and receive a membership card that you carry with you. The pass is good for one year. See: *http://www.astc.org.*

LIBRARIES

With most people downloading books on their electronic equipment, it may seem like libraries are becoming irrelevant. Combining that with the fact that many libraries will not provide a card to any but local residents may cause you to wonder why I mention libraries at all. As expressed previously, libraries are among our favorite places to visit. They provide a breath of intellectual stimulation, even if for just the afternoon. Some have fantastic displays of artwork, museums, dioramas...you might find yourself surprised at the variety of libraries there are in this country. Especially in Las Vegas, Nevada, of all places; they have art galleries, theatres and even musical performances.

Depending on the location, some libraries will offer a temporary library card for a small fee which is helpful if you plan on staying in one area for a few weeks or more. Whenever we are in an area where we do have a library card and we are getting ready for a long trip, we will often borrow a bunch of items to enjoy on the trip and snail mail them back to the library when we are done with them.

VOLUNTEER ORGANIZATIONS

I look for opportunities to do community service and volunteer wherever we can. By doing so, my son has learned about contributing in many ways including permaculture, composting, catching and caring for feral cats, plumbing, cooking, cleaning, leading small groups and working with younger children. If you do a search under "RV volunteer," you will find a number of listings.

There is also an organization that you can join to learn, live and work at organic farms around the world. World Wide Opportunities on Organic Farms (WWOOF) lists farms where people can work and stay for a while. Some farms are open to families working there. Habitat for Humanity has a volunteer program for RVers as well as the National Park Service. There are endless possibilities to live and volunteer. Here are a few to start with:

http://www.habitat.org/rv
http://www.wwoofusa.org
https://www.volunteer.gov/results.cfm

8. TRIP PLANNING TOOLS AND THEMES

S ome people prefer to roadschool in short spurts while others opt for lengthy stretches. Your personal style for adventure will likely depend at least in part on your budget for time and finances. Whether you have a themed trip in mind, want to select specific spots or prefer to let the road guide your journey, any time spent roadschooling is worth the effort. Here are some options for making the most of your adventure.

TYPES OF TRAVEL

Thanks to the Interstate Highway System, it is now possible to travel across the country from coast to coast without seeing anything. – Charles Kuralt

When I had less time, I covered many miles and spent more money. Those days were pretty action-packed and well-planned in advance. I didn't want to miss out on anything that was near our itinerary! Now that we are out here all the time, I don't rush as much as I used to. I figured out quickly that if we like an area, we can stay there for a little while to thoroughly explore and absorb it before moving on. The advantage to this type of travel is that it not only enables you to learn more about each location, it also allows you to make new friends, to find new volunteer experiences and enroll in classes, groups or ongoing events of interest. When it comes time to leave, I will often plan ahead for the next volunteer experience so we have a place to land once we decide what part of the country we wish to explore next.

PLANNING YOUR TRIPS

All journeys have secret destinations of which the traveler is unaware. – Martin Buber

I like to do a bunch of preparation and planning for most of our trips. This doesn't mean that I cannot be sidetracked, but I am less likely to miss out on something unique if I take the time to do the research beforehand. If you are a careful planner, you can often find low-cost or free places to park on the way to your favorite destinations.

Besides looking for great spots to visit through the internet, there are a couple of other resources that I would never plan a trip without. Every year, I purchase a new road atlas of the United States. This may seem unnecessary since I use a GPS when traveling, but the road map lists attractions in red that I would not see on my GPS. Although most road atlases have extra sights listed on them, my favorite is the one put out by Michelin because it has an abundance of interesting places to explore. I also would never plan a trip without consulting a recent copy of *National Geographic's Scenic Highways*. Also see *https://www.tripadvisor.com*.

TRAVEL THEMES

Themed trips can be a fabulous learning tool. We have done a few of them including a "Swamp Trip" one year where we visited different kinds of swamps and learned all about them. We have also taken a trip along the wagon trail that runs from Ohio across the west. The old road is still there with statues to honor all the people who traveled by wagon in the 1800's. And because Rockett was a dinosaur enthusiast even before we began roadschooling, visiting prehistoric sites has been a priority. There are so many topics to explore along the road: the Santa Fe Trail, Dinosaur Diamond, Lewis and Clark's Journey, the Trail of Tears, animal migrations and loads of history themes to embark upon. You can be as creative as your family's interests allow you to be. Don't forget to bring audio books to enhance your journey.

INVITE COMPANY

It can be really fun to have your loved ones join you for a part of your journey. Although most people may not be able to get away for long periods of time, they can often take a short trip to meet you somewhere. A good friend of ours has met up with us at certain points along the way. A few times we picked her up at one airport and then dropped her several hundred miles along our journey at another airport. Those are some of our favorite travel memories. Even if friends or family cannot join you on your trip, they can join you in spirit by following you on a map and keeping in contact with you through internet and cell connections.

9. LASTING THOUGHTS

People who don't travel cannot have a global view; all they see is what's in front of them. Those people cannot accept new things because all they know is where they live. –
Martin Yan

Rockett and I are still enjoying our roadschooling journey. We would suggest a few things be kept in mind as you ponder the possibilities for your family. Make sure that you have a good support system before you go. I would not be able to roadschool if we did not have such caring people in our lives. If you find that some folks disagree with your plans, don't worry; they might change their tune when they see how your children blossom from their roadschooling experiences. And if those folks don't, that's okay...perhaps they can be supportive down the road if you decide to return and get settled again.

Let your children participate and lead the way with trip planning as much as possible. Not only is doing so more likely to keep their interest and attention, doors are opened more easily for children than adults. For example, because Rockett was interested in dinosaurs, I asked a curator at one museum in Utah if he wouldn't mind meeting my son, a young dinosaur enthusiast. It turned out that this person was an expert dinosaur anthropologist and he gave us a private tour of the rest of the museum AND brought us into the back room so that Rockett could feed their alligator.

Be sure that the kids enjoy the places you are visiting. I like it when I have something cool to look forward to when I get my studies done. I also like having my own special job when it comes to setting up our RV. I handle the water and hookups. It makes me feel good to help out.

One of the joys of parenthood is to give the gift of enjoying life to the fullest. Remember, humans have been nomads for millennia, so this is part of our nature. We are with our children for such a short time. Be sure to listen to your intuition, treasure the moments, take LOTS of pictures and if a special opportunity or invitation comes your way, go for it!

RESOURCES

- *Guide to Scenic Highways & Byways*, National Geographic, Washington, D.C.
- *Michelin Road Atlas (Most recent version.)*
- *http://www.nps.gov*
- *http://gorving.com/*
- *www.abrome.com*
- *http://www.coolworks.com/jobs-with-rv-spaces/*
- *http://www.work-for-rvers-and-campers.com/*
- *http://www.roadworking.com/rver-jobs.html*
- *https://www.workamper.com/*
- *http://www.amazonfulfillmentcareers.com/opportunities/camper-force/*
- *www.Goodsamclub.com*
- *www.passportamerica.com*
- *https://escapees.com*
- *http://www.astc.org*
- *https://meridiansofhealth.com/upcoming-events/wild-herb-week/*
- *ww.aaa.com*
- *http://www.habitat.org/rv*
- *http://www.wwoofusa.org*
- *https://www.volunteer.gov/results.cfm*
- *https://www.tripadvisor.com*
- *http://www.travelinghomeschoolers.com/*

INDEX

Made in the USA
Columbia, SC
23 April 2017